CALGARY PUBLIC LIBRARY
NOVEMBER 2019

KAWAII
CRAFT LIFE

Super-Cute Projects

for Home, Work & Play

SOSAE CAETANO AND DENNIS CAETANO

RUNNING PRESS
PHILADELPHIA

Running Press
Hachette Book Group
1290 Avenue of the Americas, New York, NY 10104
www.runningpress.com
@Running_Press

Printed in China
First Edition: May 2019

Published by Running Press, an imprint of Perseus Books, LLC,
a subsidiary of Hachette Book Group, Inc.

The Hachette Speakers Bureau provides a wide range of authors for speaking events.
To find out more, go to www.hachettespeakersbureau.com or call (866) 376-6591.

The publisher is not responsible for websites
(or their content) that are not owned by the publisher.

Prop styling by Kristi Hunter
Print book cover and interior design by Susan Van Horn

Library of Congress Control Number: 2018955315
ISBNs: 978-0-7624-9381-4 (paperback), 978-0-7624-9379-1 (ebook)

RRD-S

10 9 8 7 6 5 4 3 2

contents

Introduction...1

Needlecraft Essentials...3

Stitch Library...10

FELTCRAFT...13

COUNTED CROSS-STITCH...85

EMBROIDERY...119

introduction

WHAT IS KAWAII?

Simply put, kawaii is the aesthetic of all things cheerful, sweet, and adorable. The word *kawaii* means "cute" in Japanese. But it's so much more than that. Kawaii is about seeing the bright side of life, and it has the power to make you smile. (Yes, the same disarming power that babies and little animals have!) It's the precious, the cuddly, the silly, and the imperfect. Kawaii is all things super-cute.

NEEDLECRAFT

Needlecraft is as old as time, and yet it's forever modern. That's because there's no end to the wonderful things you can create with a needle and thread. These days, stitching is a perfect antidote to technology overload. Once you pick up needle and thread, you're only a few stitches away from a lower heart rate, calmer breathing, and a more tranquil mind. And we should also note: Stitching is fun. A *lot* of fun.

A BIT ABOUT US

We started our needlecraft journey years ago, when the hurly-burly of life got to be a bit much. Crafting with needle and thread quickly became an empowering way to deal with stress, to unwind, and to express our creativity. And, of course, we've always loved kawaii style—long before we even knew what kawaii was! Our first hand-stitched kawaii felt plushie—a sweet and dreamy blue cloud—inspired us to design even more needlecraft projects. And design we did: from felt animals to whimsical cottage ornaments and kawaii monsters. We made digital instant-download patterns of all our designs and launched our pattern company, Trellis & Thyme.

   Since then, we've created over 140 patterns, and that's just the beginning. Inspiration strikes us every day and we're always designing, sketching, and playing with ideas for the next project. Whether we're creating a pattern or stitching it to life, needlecraft brings us so much happiness, and we hope it does the same for you!

ABOUT THE PROJECTS IN THIS BOOK

For this book we've designed thirty-five original kawaii projects for you to hand-stitch, cross-stitch, and embroider. Our hope is that you'll feel inspired to try some (or all!) of them. Many of the projects can be created in a single afternoon, but some will take a bit more time and patience. They all require your unique hand and style to come to life.

This book is divided into four main sections: Needlecraft Essentials, Feltcraft, Counted Cross-Stitch, and Embroidery. Needlecraft Essentials (page 3) is a wonderful introduction to the basics of hand-stitching. You'll learn all about needle, thread, fabric, and other essential tools for creating the projects in this book. Plus there's a handy Stitch Library (page 10) that shows you how to make the simple stitches that bring these projects together.

Each project in this book includes a list of materials and illustrated step-by-step instructions—some also have templates, included at the back of the book—to guide you through the making process. We want your creative time to be well-spent and, above all, fun! We've also included a few alternate colors for some of the projects, such as the Cupcake Bag Charm (page 36) and Fudge Pop Plushie (page 48). We hope this encourages you to play and choose your own color combinations. Remember, with kawaii style there is no right or wrong—just do what you love!

In writing *Kawaii Craft Life*, more than anything we wanted to show how needlecraft can be a creative and exciting way to add charm to everyday life. Almost anything can be adorned with stitches, so let your imagination run wild. For example, if you like the Dragon Bookmark design (page 136), maybe you'd rather stitch it on a pillowcase or even the back pocket of a pair of jeans. And remember, kawaii style encourages playfulness, so don't fuss with perfection.

We'd love to see your projects! Follow Trellis & Thyme on Instagram (@SosaeCaetano) and be sure to include #KawaiiCraftLife with your project posts.

So go ahead and add some kawaii charm to your life! Remember to make it silly. Make it cute. Make it wonky. Make it uniquely yours.

—*Sosae and Dennis*

Needlecraft Essentials

The projects in this book focus on feltcraft, counted cross-stitch, and embroidery. Though they share similar tools and techniques, there are still plenty of details that set these crafts apart. Get to know the essentials and have fun!

FELTCRAFT

To work with felt is to fall in love with felt. Maybe it's the rich, dense fabric that doesn't fray when you cut it. Maybe it's all the vivid felt colors, or the fact that it's so versatile you can create almost anything with it. Here are a few things to know before jumping into the wonderful world of felt.

CHOOSE YOUR FELT

ACRYLIC: This is the kind of felt you will find at big craft stores. It tends to be thin and the quality is not ideal for hand-stitched projects.

WOOL: Wool felt is a soft and dense fabric. It has an heirloom quality, which makes it perfect for hand-stitched items, and it comes in lots of rich colors. It's also rather expensive. You can find wool felt at craft stores or online.

WOOL-BLEND: This is our favorite type of felt. It feels like pure wool felt, comes in hundreds of rich colors, and is very affordable. You can find the best selection of wool-blend felt online.

FELTCRAFT TOOLS

EMBROIDERY NEEDLE: A sharp embroidery needle is a must for working with felt. They come in a variety of sizes, so choose a size that suits the project. For example, if you're stitching something quite small, you'll want to use a smaller needle (size 9 or 10). Some projects require you to stitch through more than two layers of felt at once. In those instances it may be helpful to change to a larger needle (size 5 or 6) to help poke through all the layers. (Note: Smaller needles have a larger number.)

THREAD: Six-stranded cotton embroidery floss is ideal for hand-stitching with felt. Cut a working length of about 20 inches. Most of the felt projects in this book will have you stitching with three strands of floss. Be gentle as you pull the strands apart to avoid tangles.

CRAFT SCISSORS: To cut through felt, you need a pair of sharp craft scissors. Choose a pair that has a pointed tip, as that will come in handy for cutting out tiny felt pieces.

FINE-TIP BLACK MARKING PEN: When you need to mark things on felt, a fine-tip black pen is very handy. (Avoid felt-tip pens, as they will bleed ink and the ink will spread through the felt fabric.)

FABRIC GLUE: Fabric glue comes in handy when working with felt. It's ideal for attaching small felt pieces (like Cheeks, Noses, etc.)

that would be very difficult to stitch otherwise. When applying glue to felt, use a small paintbrush to coat the surface evenly. Always let the glue dry completely before continuing with the project.

SNAP CLOSURES: Some of the projects in this book require metal snap closures. They're super-easy to sew. Simply mark their location on the felt using a fine-tip pen, then sew in place according to the manufacturer's instructions.

STITCHING WITH FELT

Stitching with felt is easy. Simply cut out the templates and felt pieces, thread your needle (making a knot at the end), and follow the simple project instructions. All the stitches you'll need for this book can be found in the Stitch Library (page 10).

COUNTED CROSS-STITCH

Cross-stitch is all the rage. It's hip, it's fun, it's relaxing, and it creates a unique and very pretty stitch-scape! *Counted* cross-stitch simply refers to a kind of cross-stitch that follows a pattern chart and uses a gridded fabric called aida.

CROSS-STITCH TOOLS

FABRIC AIDA: Aida comes in many colors and grid sizes. For the projects in this book, we recommend white 14-count aida. It's the most common type and can be found at major craft stores.

PLASTIC AIDA: Some of the projects in this book call for 14-count plastic aida. It's ideal for anything that needs to be a bit more sturdy. You can order plastic aida online or look for it at your local craft store.

NEEDLE: A dull-tip tapestry needle is best for cross-stitching. (The aida fabric already has holes in it, so you don't need a sharp needle to poke through.) Use a medium-size needle so it doesn't stretch the holes in the aida (size 24–26.)

THREAD: Cross-stitch the projects in this book using six-stranded cotton embroidery floss. Cut a working length of about 15 inches and stitch with two strands. The cross-stitch patterns in this book reference DMC floss colors.

SCISSORS: You will need a pair of sharp craft scissors to cut through fabric or plastic aida. Cutting out finished cross-stitch designs is all about precision, so make sure your scissors have a pointed tip.

HOW TO READ A CROSS-STITCH CHART

In this book, cross-stitch charts feature solid color blocks for quick and easy reference. Each color block corresponds to a DMC floss color as well as a position on the aida fabric.

HOW TO CROSS-STITCH

Remember to cross-stitch using only two strands of embroidery floss. Most of the projects in this book require aida pieces that are too small for a hoop, which is just fine because aida is great to hold and stitch as is.

Before you begin, it's helpful to locate the center of your aida. Once you know the approximate center, you can count over to your chosen starting point on the cross-stitch design chart.

Cross-stitches are done in two parts: First you will make a series of half cross-stitches, and then you will return to complete each one. Here's how you begin: Start by bringing your needle up through the aida at point 1 (leaving a 1-inch "tail" of floss in the back). Bring your needle down to point 2. Come back up at point 3 and back down at point 4. Repeat for the entire column.

To complete the cross-stitches, come up at point 9 and go back down at point 10. Then come up at point 11 and go back down at point 12. Repeat until you've completed all the cross-stitches in the column.

When changing threads' or finishing, simply weave the working floss into a few stitches on the back of your aida and cut. (Unlike in hand-stitching and embroidery, in cross-stitch you do not tie off with a knot. All ends are woven in to existing stitches for a smooth, flat finish.)

A quick and gentle press with an iron will remove any creases from finished cross-stitch designs that are stitched on fabric aida. Place a cloth over the aida as you press (or press on the opposite side of the design) and remember to

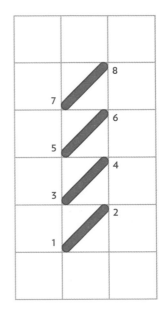

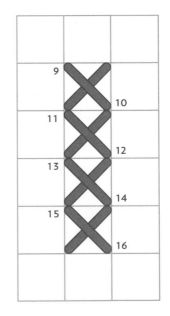

be very gentle so as not to flatten the stitches. If the project calls for cutting out the design, do so carefully with a pair of pointed-tip scissors. Cut one full square away from the design's edge, leaving an aida border around the design. (If you cut any closer, you will break the grid and your stitches will come undone.) Note: Never iron plastic aida—it will melt!

TIPS: Take a break and wash your hands periodically as you stitch. This will keep your stitchwork clean. Avoid using any lotion before or during your stitchwork, as the oils can be absorbed into your work and cause stains.

If your aida or embroidery fabric has a small stain, soak it in a warm bath with a drop or two of mild laundry detergent. Rinse under a gentle stream of water, being careful not to agitate the stitchwork. Press out excess water between two towels (do not wring!) and lay flat to dry. (Note: Do not wash felt because it will shrink!)

EMBROIDERY

Embroidery is both fun and pretty. You can embroider on anything, from aprons to cotton napkins, felt pencil cases to knit onesies. It's a way of bringing fabric to life, by adorning it with precious handmade stitches.

EMBROIDERY TOOLS

NEEDLE: A sharp embroidery needle is necessary for embroidering on felt or other fabric. Make sure you have a few different sizes on hand, but in general, it's best to stitch with a midsize needle (size 7–9). (The larger the needle, the larger the hole it makes in your fabric.)

THREAD: Six-stranded cotton embroidery floss is ideal for embroidering the projects in this book. Use three of the six strands when stitching. Cut a working length of about 20 inches. The embroidery designs in this book reference DMC thread colors, but feel free to choose whatever colors you love most.

SCISSORS: Embroidery scissors come in all kinds of beautiful shapes and colors. The one thing they have in common is how sharp they are. You need a pair of small sharp scissors that can easily cut little threads.

MARKING PENS: A fine-tip black pen is ideal for transferring embroidery designs onto felt or other fabric. For marking on dark felt, use a white, fine-tip, oil-based paint pen. (Both can be found at office supply and craft stores.)

HOOPS: Embroidery hoops come in many different sizes. Choose a size that suits your project. When stitching with an embroidery hoop, it's best not to tighten it too much. A too-tight hoop can damage your fabric. Also, be sure to remove your project from the hoop whenever you're done stitching for the day to prevent permanent creases. The only time you want to really tighten the embroidery hoop is when you're using it as a frame to display a finished project.

THIMBLE: Some people like using a thimble when they stitch to help push the needle through the fabric. Experiment with metal or rubber thimbles to see what you like best.

HOW TO EMBROIDER

The most important step in embroidery is getting the design onto your fabric. (See the transfer guide to your right for more information.) Once the design has been transferred, place your fabric in a hoop or, in the case of felt and other thick fabrics, simply hold it in your hand. Thread your needle, make a small knot on the end, and poke upward through the underside of the fabric. Based on the project's instructions, choose an appropriate stitch from the Stitch Library (page 10), reference a color chart if necessary, and follow the design on the fabric. It's that simple.

If your embroidery is done on fabric, you can either soak it in a warm bath to relax the hoop creases, or just give it a gentle press with the iron on the opposite side of the design. Do not iron felt—it can shrink or melt.

DESIGN TRANSFER TECHNIQUES

Whether you're stitching a teacup on a flour-sack towel or a cheerful face on a felt fudge pop plushie, you need a way of getting the design onto your fabric. Read through the following transfer techniques and choose the best one for your particular project.

WINDOW: This is the classic design transfer tool for lightweight fabric. Simply take your design template and tape it to a sunny window. Then place your fabric over it, tape it, and proceed to trace the design onto your fabric using a fine-tip pen.

LIGHTBOX/LIGHTPAD: A lightbox/lightpad is a wonderful tool to have if you plan on embroidering often. With strong light settings, it works well for transferring on all sorts of fabric, including cotton canvas and light-colored felt.

TISSUE PAPER: Trace the design onto white tissue paper. Then pin the tissue paper to your fabric and stitch through it. When you're done, gently tear the tissue paper away.

PIN-POKE TECHNIQUE: This is one of our favorite transfer techniques. It's suitable for transferring small designs (like face details) and even complex ones onto felt or any fabric. Once you've photocopied your embroidery design template, take a sharp pin and carefully poke holes through the design at $1/8$-inch intervals. When your design template looks like Swiss cheese, you're ready to transfer. (Note: It's very important that your template not move during the transfer process, so be sure to pin it to your fabric!) With a fine-tip pen, mark tiny dots through the holes you made in the design. When you're finished, you should have a lovely connect-the-dots transfer to stitch over.

Pin-Poke Technique

Stitch Library

All the projects in this book can be created by learning a few simple stitches. Whether you're hand-stitching a felt plushie or embroidering on a soft cotton napkin, the techniques are simple and fun to learn.

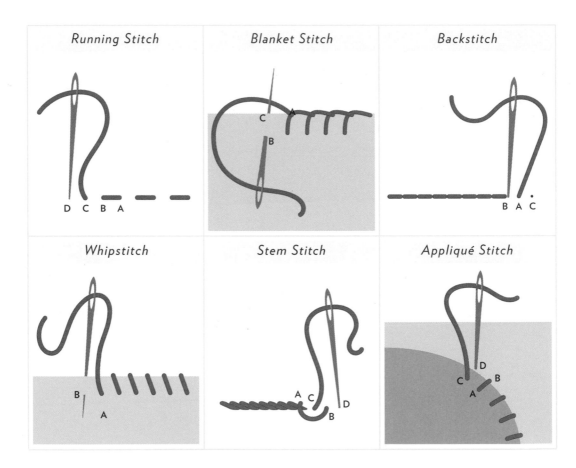

RUNNING STITCH: This is a very simple stitch to make. It looks best when the stitches are even in length and evenly spaced.

Bring the needle up through the fabric at point A, then back down at point B. Come back up at point C, and go back down at point D. Repeat.

BLANKET STITCH: This stitch is used throughout this book for stitching the edges of felt together, and for attaching Ears, Feet, Tails, etc. between felt pieces. It creates a pretty edging and is also quite fun to do.

From point A, insert your needle into the fabric at point B, keeping the thread behind the needle at point C. Tug to tighten thread and repeat.

BACKSTITCH: This is a very versatile stitch, most often used for outlining. Most embroidery designs can be stitched entirely in backstitch. We love it for its simplicity and clean lines. To create smooth curves with backstitch, shorten the stitch length.

Bring your needle up through the fabric at point A, then go back down at point B, and come back up through the bottom at point C. Repeat.

WHIPSTITCH: This stitch is a clean and simple way to bind the edges of felt together. It's best to keep your stitches compact and even.

Go through both layers of felt at point A, then around the edge of the felt to insert through the other side at point B. Tug the thread gently to tighten, and repeat.

STEM STITCH: This stitch is perfect for making smooth, curvy lines. It creates a thicker outline than backstitch.

Come up through the fabric at point A, but keep the thread loose as you go down into point B. (It helps to put your finger on the thread to keep it from pulling all the way through.) Come back up at point C, then go back down into the fabric at point D, and pull the thread snug.

APPLIQUÉ STITCH: This technique is used throughout the book for stitching one piece of felt flatly atop another. It's best to keep your stitches small and neat.

Come up through both layers of felt at point A and go back down just off the edge of the top felt at point B. Then come back up through both layers at point C and go back down off the edge of the top felt again at point D. Repeat.

FELTCRAFT

TOASTER PASTRY GIFT CARD HOLDER

Toaster pastries aren't just for breakfast anymore. Traditionally stuffed with fruity filling, this frosted kawaii pastry holds something sweeter—a gift card! It's so easy to stitch that you'll want to make a dozen of them. And don't just stop at gift cards, either: Make one for your purse, bag, or backpack to hold your business cards or all your other important cards.

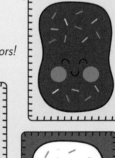

Mix and match felt colors to create your own unique toaster pastry flavors!

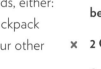*materials*

- ✗ **Frosting: 3" x 4" white felt**

- ✗ **Front and Back Pastry: 8" x 5" cream felt**

- ✗ **Embroidery floss in the following colors: beige, white, pink, black**

- ✗ **2 Cheeks: 1" x 2" pink felt**

- ✗ **Small rainbow-colored bugle beads for sprinkles (about 15)**

- ✗ **Scissors**

- ✗ **Straight pins**

- ✗ **Embroidery needle**

- ✗ **Marking pen**

- ✗ **Fabric glue**

- ✗ **Small paintbrush**

Cut out the templates (page 158). Pin the templates to the felt pieces, and cut carefully along the lines. Once you've cut out all the felt pieces, you're ready to begin!

Use 3 strands of embroidery floss to stitch this project.

1> Position the Frosting onto the Front Pastry felt. Appliqué stitch it in place with matching thread.

2> Mark Eyes and Mouth on the Frosting felt with a marking pen. Use black thread to backstitch the face detail. Appliqué stitch the Cheeks in place with matching thread or glue them in place with fabric glue.

3> Stitch bugle bead "sprinkles" randomly onto the Frosting using white thread.

4> Align the Front and Back Pastry felt and pin them together. With darker thread, blanket stitch the two together, starting at the bottom and stopping at the top right corner.

5> Once you reach the top right corner, blanket stitch along the top edge of the Front Pastry only. (This will leave the top open for inserting your gift card!)

6> When you've reached the top left corner, continue to blanket stitch both the Front and Back Pastry felt together until finished. Fasten off.

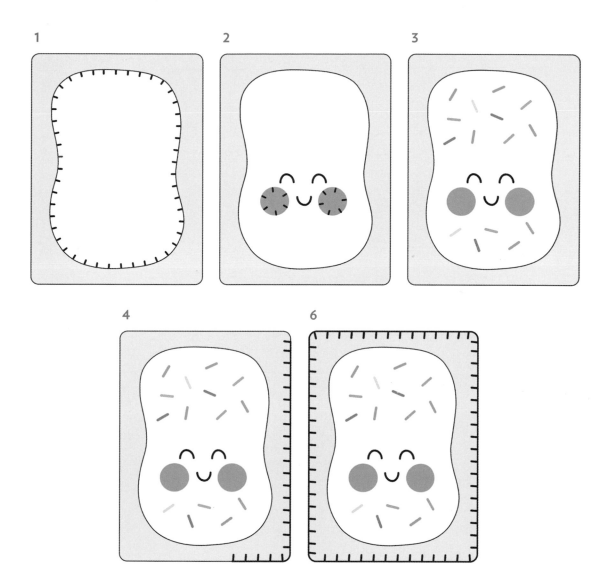

RAINBOW CLOUD PLUSHIE

This is one pretty plushie! On one side you have Dreamy Cloud, looking all sweet and sleepy and ready for bed. On the other side it's Happy Cloud, with a bright rainbow and all the enthusiasm needed to start the day. This is a project you will love to stitch, and you'll have it finished in no time. The best part is having a Rainbow Cloud plushie to adorn your bed, couch, or any place at all.

materials

× **Dreamy Cloud Side:** 6″ x 8″ white felt

× **Embroidery floss in the following colors:** white, blue, hot pink, orange, yellow, green, light pink, black

× **4 Cheeks:** 1″ x 2″ pink felt

× **Happy Cloud Side:** 7½″ x 3½″ white felt

× **Sky:** 6″ x 8″ light blue felt

× **Pink Band:** 5″ x 4″ pink felt

× **Orange Band:** 3″ x 4″ orange felt

× **Yellow Band:** 3½″ x 2½″ yellow felt

× **Green Band:** 2½″ x 2½″ green felt

× **Poly-fill stuffing**

× **Scissors**

× **Straight pins**

× **Marking pen**

× **Embroidery needle**

× **Fabric glue**

× **Small paintbrush**

Cut out the templates (page 159). Pin the templates to the felt pieces, and cut carefully along the lines. Once you've cut out all the felt pieces, you're ready to begin!

Use 3 strands of embroidery floss to stitch this project.

1 ⟩ Mark the Eyes and the Mouth on the Dreamy Cloud felt with a marking pen. Use black thread to backstitch the face detail. Appliqué stitch the Cheeks in place with matching thread or glue them in place with fabric glue. Set aside.

2 ⟩ Mark the Eyes and Mouth on the Happy Cloud felt with a marking pen. Use black thread to backstitch the mouth. Appliqué stitch or glue the Eyes in place with fabric glue. Appliqué stitch the Cheeks in place. Set aside.

3 ⟩ Place the Pink Band atop the Sky felt, about ½" in from the top edge. Pin in place. With matching thread, appliqué stitch along the top only.

4 ⟩ Place the Orange Band atop the Sky felt, overlapping the Pink Band by about ¼". Pin in place. With matching thread, appliqué stitch along the top only. Repeat for the Yellow Band and the Green Band.

5 ⟩ Place the Happy Cloud atop the Sky felt, overlapping the rainbow. Pin the felt and appliqué stitch in place with matching thread.

6 ⟩ Align the Dreamy Cloud and the Sky felt, back to back, and pin them together. Using a brightly colored thread, blanket stitch them together, starting near the top left. When you're about 2" away from where you started, begin stuffing with poly-fill. Once the Rainbow Cloud has reached your desired poofiness, continue to blanket stitch shut.

1

2

3

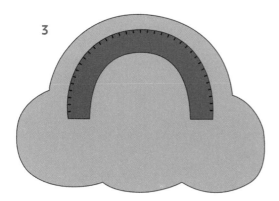

4

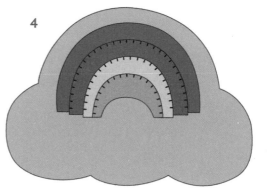

5

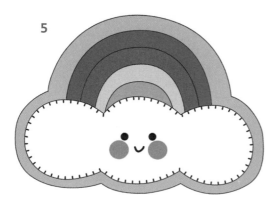

6

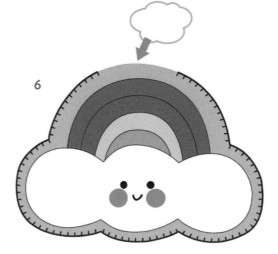

FAST FOOD KEYCHAINS

What's better than a juicy burger, a box of golden fries, and a frosty milk shake? These adorable fast food keychains, of course! Super-fun to stitch, they're perfect for the calorie-conscious, or as an homage to this iconic fast food trio. And because they're so bright and so much fun to carry, you'll never have to worry about losing your keys again!

materials

- ✗ 3 metal key rings
- ✗ 24" length baker's twine
- ✗ Embroidery floss in the following colors: beige, red, blue, white, black
- ✗ Poly-fill stuffing
- ✗ Scissors
- ✗ Straight pins
- ✗ Marking pen
- ✗ Fabric glue
- ✗ Small paintbrush
- ✗ Embroidery needle

FRIES

- ✗ **Box Front and Back: 5" x 3" red felt**
- ✗ **Fries: 2½" x 3" yellow felt**
- ✗ **2 Cheeks: 1" x 2" pink felt**

SHAKE

- ✗ **Label: 2" x 3" white felt**
- ✗ **Cup: 3" x 3" blue felt**
- ✗ **Lid: 1" x 3" white felt**
- ✗ **Straw: 1" x 2" pink felt**
- ✗ **2 Cheeks: 1" x 2" pink felt**
- ✗ **Backing: 4" x 4" dark pink felt**

BURGER

- ✗ **Top Bun: 2" x 3½" beige felt**
- ✗ **Lettuce: 1" x 3½" green felt**
- ✗ **Tomato: 1" x 3½" red felt**
- ✗ **Cheese: 1" x 3½" yellow felt**
- ✗ **Patty: 1" x 3½" brown felt**
- ✗ **Bottom Bun: 1" x 3½" beige felt**
- ✗ **Backing: 4" x 3½" dark pink felt**
- ✗ **2 Cheeks: 1" x 2" pink felt**

For each keychain you will need an 8″ length of baker's twine and a key ring. Knot both ends of the twine together, leaving a large loop. Insert the loop through the key ring and pull the knot end through the loop.

Cut out the templates (pages 160–161). Pin the templates to the felt pieces, and cut carefully along the lines. Once you've cut out all the felt pieces, you're ready to begin!

Use 3 strands of embroidery floss to stitch this project.

FRIES

1 〉 Mark the Eyes and Mouth on the Box Front felt with a marking pen. Use black thread to backstitch the face detail. Glue the Cheeks in place with fabric glue.

2 〉 Align the Box Front and Back felt, and pin them together. Using matching thread, blanket stitch the two together starting at the bottom right. When you reach the top right, insert the Fries between the Front and Back felt, and continue to stitch through to secure the Fries in place. When you reach the top center, insert the twine (knot down)

between the Front and Back felt, behind the Fries. (Be sure your stitches catch the knot to secure the twine.) Continue to blanket stitch until you reach the bottom left. Gently stuff with poly-fill and blanket stitch shut.

1

2

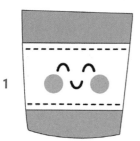

1

2

4

SHAKE

1 > Mark the Eyes and Mouth on the Label felt with a marking pen. Position the Label onto the Cup felt and pin them together. With brightly colored thread, backstitch along the top and bottom of the Label. Backstitch the face detail using black thread. Glue the Cheeks in place with fabric glue.

2 > Place the Lid atop the Cup felt, overlapping by about ¼". Glue the Lid in place with fabric glue.

3 > Place the Cup atop the Backing felt, and pin them together. Carefully cut along the edges until you have a perfectly matched backing piece. Do not remove the pins.

4 > Using matching thread, blanket stitch the Cup and the Backing felt together, starting at the bottom right, removing the pins as you go. When you reach the top right, insert the Straw between the Cup and the Backing felt, and continue to stitch through to secure it in place. Continue another one or two blanket stitches until you reach the top center. Insert the twine (knot down) between the Cup and the Backing felt. (Be sure your stitches catch the knot to secure the twine.) Continue to blanket stitch until you reach the bottom left. Gently stuff with poly-fill and blanket stitch shut.

BURGER

1 > Mark the Eyes and Mouth on the Top Bun felt, using a marking pen. Use black thread to backstitch the face detail. Glue the Cheeks in place with fabric glue.

2 > Glue the Cheese felt, slightly overlapping the Patty felt. Glue the Tomato felt, slightly overlapping the Cheese felt. Glue the Lettuce felt, slightly overlapping the Tomato felt.

3 > Glue the Top Bun, slightly overlapping the Lettuce felt. Glue the Bottom Bun, slightly overlapping the Patty felt.

4 > Place the Burger atop the Backing felt, and pin them together. Carefully cut along the edges until you have a perfectly matched backing piece. Do not remove the pins.

5 > Using matching thread, blanket stitch the Burger and Backing felt together, starting at the bottom right, removing the pins as you go. When you reach the top center, insert the twine (knot down) between the Top Bun and the Backing felt. (Be sure your stitches catch the knot to secure the twine.) Continue to blanket stitch until you reach the bottom left. Gently stuff with poly-fill and blanket stitch shut.

1

2

3

4

NARWHAL BROOCH

The magical narwhal comes to life in this lovely little project. With his bright eyes, pink cheeks, and golden tusk, this narwhal brooch will quickly become your favorite adornment. Simple and quick to stitch, you may also want to create a colorful pod of narwhals for pinning on jackets, backpacks, hats, or any place that needs a nautical kawaii touch.

materials

- ✕ **2 Eyes: 1″ x 1″ black felt**
- ✕ **Front and Back Body: 5″ x 3″ light blue felt**
- ✕ **Embroidery floss in the following colors: light blue, yellow, pink, black**
- ✕ **2 Cheeks: 1″ x 1″ pink felt**
- ✕ **Tusk: 1″ x 1″ yellow felt**
- ✕ **Flippers and Tail: 3″ x 3″ light blue felt**
- ✕ **Small Rectangle: 1″ x 1″ light blue felt**
- ✕ **Medium-size safety pin**
- ✕ **Poly-fill stuffing**
- ✕ **Scissors**
- ✕ **Straight pins**
- ✕ **Marking pen**
- ✕ **Fabric glue**
- ✕ **Small paintbrush**

Cut out the templates (page 161). Pin the templates to the felt pieces, and cut carefully along the lines. Once you've cut out all the felt pieces, you're ready to begin!

Use 3 strands of embroidery floss to stitch this project.

1 > Mark the Eyes and Mouth on the Front Body felt with a marking pen. Use black thread to backstitch the Mouth. Glue the Eyes in place with fabric glue. Appliqué stitch the Cheeks in place with matching thread or glue them in place with fabric glue.

2 > With matching thread, appliqué stitch the Tusk along the bottom only. With matching thread, appliqué stitch the Right Flipper along the top only. Set aside.

3 > Center the Small Rectangle onto the Back Body piece. Appliqué stitch it in place along the bottom, insert the safety pin, then appliqué stitch the top to secure the safety pin in place.

4 > Align the Front and Back Body pieces, back to back, and pin them together. Starting in the upper right, whipstitch them together with matching thread. When you reach the spot just below the Cheeks on the left, insert the Left Flipper between the two Body pieces and continue to whipstitch through it, securing it in place. Repeat the same process for the Tail.

5 > When you're about 1" away from where you started in step 4, lightly stuff with poly-fill. Continue to whipstitch shut.

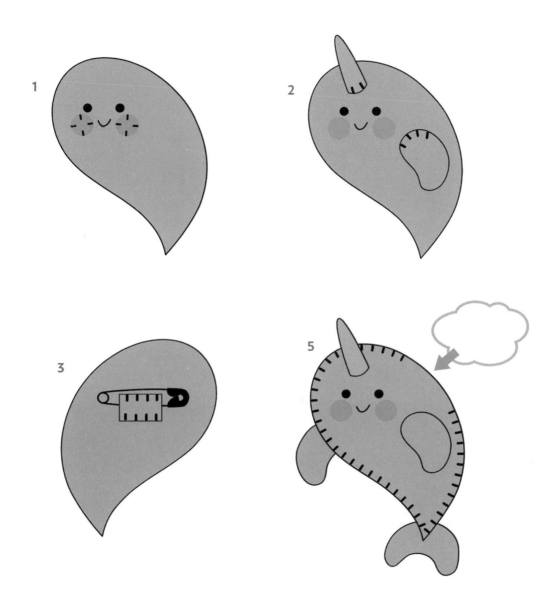

GLAM PINEAPPLE PLUSHIE

Pineapples are the rock stars of fruit, and this glam pineapple is the leader of the band! With sparkly gold sequins and a top of spiky green leaves, this plushie will jazz up any room. The stitched stars are fun to create, and everything comes together so quickly, you may want to make a whole bunch of this good-fortune fruit.

materials

x **Pineapple Front and Back: 5″ x 10″ golden yellow felt**

x **Embroidery floss in the following colors: green, pink, and black**

x **2 Cheeks: 1″ x 2″ pink felt**

x **Gold sequins (about 6)**

x **Leaves: 3″ x 3″ green felt**

x **Poly-fill stuffing**

x **Scissors**

x **Straight pins**

x **Marking pen**

x **Embroidery needle**

x **Fabric glue**

x **Small paintbrush**

Cut out the templates (page 162). Pin the templates to the felt pieces, and cut carefully along the lines. Once you've cut out all the felt pieces, you're ready to begin!

Use 3 strands of embroidery floss to stitch this project.

1 > Mark the Eyes and Mouth on the Pineapple Front felt with a marking pen. Use black thread to backstitch the face detail. Appliqué stitch the Cheeks in place with matching thread or glue them in place with fabric glue.

2 > Mark the stars on the Pineapple Front felt with a marking pen. Sew a single sequin onto the center of each star detail. Backstitch each star detail with green thread.

3 > Align the Pineapple Front and Back felt, and pin them together. Using green thread, blanket stitch the two together, starting at the bottom right and working counterclockwise. When you reach the top right, insert the Leaves between the Front and Back felt, and continue to blanket stitch through to secure the Leaves in place.

4 > Continue to blanket stitch until you reach the bottom left. Gently stuff with poly-fill and blanket stitch shut.

1

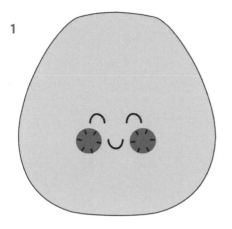

2

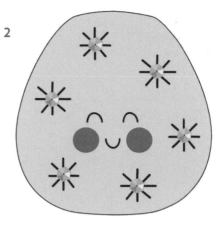

3

4

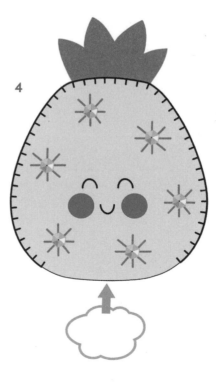

CUPCAKE BAG CHARM

Dress up your favorite handbag with this yummy kawaii cupcake charm! With her buttercream frosting and colorful sprinkles, she's too sweet not to love. A fun and simple project, you can have fun choosing unique cupcake "flavors"! A lovely ribbon and lobster clasp detail mean you can clip her to your favorite bag, or anywhere else.

Mix and match felt colors to create your own unique cupcake bag charm flavors!

materials

× **Cup: 3½" x 2½" pink felt**

× **Embroidery floss in the following colors: light pink, medium pink, dark pink, cream, mint, black**

× **2 Cheeks: 1" x 2" pink felt**

× **Cake: 3½" x 2" cream felt**

× **Frosting: 3½" x 2½" mint felt**

× **Backing: 3½" x 4" dark pink felt**

× **5" length ribbon**

× **Lobster clasp**

× **Poly-fill stuffing**

× **Scissors**

× **Straight pins**

× **Marking pen**

× **Embroidery needle**

× **Fabric glue**

× **Small paintbrush**

Cut out the templates (page 163). Pin the templates to the felt pieces, and cut carefully along the lines. Once you've cut out all the felt pieces, you're ready to begin!

Use 3 strands of embroidery floss to stitch this project.

1. Mark the eyes, mouth, and cup detail on the Cup felt, using a marking pen. Use black thread to backstitch the face detail. Use matching thread to backstitch the cup detail. With matching thread, appliqué stitch or glue the Cheeks in place.

2. Place the Cake felt over the Cup felt, overlapping by about ¼". Pin them together. Appliqué stitch the Cake to the Cup felt, using thread to match the Cake.

3. Mark the frosting detail on the Frosting felt with a marking pen, and backstitch with matching thread. Place the Frosting felt over the Cake felt, overlapping by about ¼". Pin them together. Appliqué stitch the Frosting to the Cake felt, using thread to match the Frosting.

4. Stitch small "sprinkles" onto the top of the Frosting, using various colors of thread.

5. Place the Cupcake atop the Backing felt, and pin them together. Carefully cut along the edges until you have a perfectly matched backing piece. Do not remove the pins.

6. Using a brightly colored thread, blanket stitch the Cupcake and Backing together, starting at the bottom right, removing the pins as you go. Stop when you're about ½" away from the top of the frosting. Cut a 5" length of ribbon and feed it through the ring on the lobster clasp. Bring the two ends of the ribbon together and insert between the Cupcake and Backing felt. Continue stitching to secure the ribbon.

7. When you're about 2" away from where you started, stuff gently with poly-fill. Once the Cupcake has reached your desired poofiness, blanket stitch shut.

TACO AND PIZZA PAPER CLIP TOPPERS

Who knew organizing could be so much fun? Featuring jumbo paper clips, Taco and Pizza are two very helpful office buddies! They're ready to help sort, file, and hold together your favorite projects and paperwork. Alternatively, hang them on a corkboard to display art and photos, or use as chip clips for your favorite snack. With the help of fabric glue and just a bit of stitching, this project comes together in a snap.

materials

- ✕ Black embroidery floss
- ✕ 2 jumbo paper clips
- ✕ Scissors
- ✕ Straight pins
- ✕ Marking pen
- ✕ Embroidery needle
- ✕ Fabric glue
- ✕ Small paintbrush

PIZZA

- ✕ **Pizza: 3″ x 3″ bright yellow felt**
- ✕ **2 Cheeks: 1″ x 2″ pink felt**
- ✕ **Pepperoni: red scrap felt**
- ✕ **Crust: 1″ x 3″ orange felt**
- ✕ **Backing: 3″ x 3″ yellow-orange felt**
- ✕ **Clip Cover: 2″ x 2″ yellow-orange felt**

TACO

- ✕ **Taco Front and Back: 4″ x 3″ yellow-orange felt**
- ✕ **2 Cheeks: 1″ x 2″ pink felt**
- ✕ **Tomato: 2″ x 3″ red felt**
- ✕ **Lettuce: 2″ x 3″ green felt**
- ✕ **Clip Cover: 2″ x 2″ yellow-orange felt**

Cut out the templates (page 164). Pin the templates to the felt pieces, and cut carefully along the lines. Once you've cut out all the felt pieces, you're ready to begin!

Use 3 strands of embroidery floss to stitch this project.

PIZZA

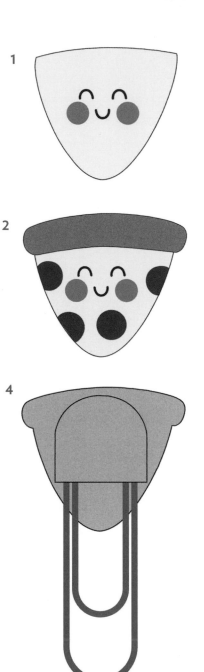

1 〉 Mark the Eyes and Mouth on the Pizza felt with a marking pen. Use black thread to backstitch the face detail. Glue the Cheeks in place with fabric glue.

2 〉 Arrange the Pepperoni as shown and glue it in place. Place the Crust felt over the Pizza felt, overlapping by about ¼", and glue it in place.

3 〉 Place the Pizza atop the Backing felt and pin them together. Carefully cut along the edges until you have a perfectly matched backing piece. Glue the Pizza and the Backing felt together.

4 〉 Glue the paper clip to the Backing felt. Let it dry. Glue the Clip Cover over the paper clip, pressing firmly to help the felt conform to the shape of the paper clip. Let it dry completely before using, about 20 minutes.

TACO

1 ⟩ Mark the Eyes and Mouth on the Taco Front felt with a marking pen. Use black thread to backstitch the face detail. Glue the Cheeks in place.

2 ⟩ Glue the Tomato felt to the back of the Taco felt, allowing it to peek just over the top.

3 ⟩ Glue the Lettuce felt to the back of the Tomato felt, again allowing it to peek just over the top.

4 ⟩ Glue the Taco Back to the Lettuce felt.

5 ⟩ Glue the paper clip to the Taco Back felt. Let it dry. Glue the Clip Cover over the paper clip, pressing firmly to help the felt conform to the shape of the paper clip. Let it dry completely before using, about 20 minutes.

43

LITTLE CRAB CORD KEEPER

Little Crab likes to keep things tidy, and tangled device cords are his pet peeve. If knotted headphone wires and twisted USB cords are making you crabby, too, then you'll definitely want to stitch a Little Crab Cord Keeper of your own. His soft shell features a snappy closure that will help keep small cords organized and tangle-free.

materials

- ✗ **Crab Shell: 5″ x 6″ orange felt**

- ✗ **Embroidery floss in the following colors: dark orange, pink, black**

- ✗ **2 Cheeks: 1″ x 2″ pink felt**

- ✗ **Claws and Legs: 4″ x 4″ dark orange felt**

- ✗ **Snap closure (in 2 parts)**

- ✗ **Crab Lining: 5″ x 6″ dark orange felt**

- ✗ **Scissors**

- ✗ **Straight pins**

- ✗ **Marking pen**

- ✗ **Embroidery needle**

- ✗ **Fabric glue**

- ✗ **Small paintbrush**

Cut out the templates (page 165). Pin templates to the felt pieces, and cut carefully along the lines. Once you've cut out all the felt pieces, you're ready to begin!

Use 3 strands of embroidery floss to stitch this project.

1 > Mark the Eyes and Mouth on the Crab Shell felt. Use black thread to backstitch the face detail. Appliqué stitch the Cheeks in place with matching thread or use glue to secure them in place.

2 > With matching thread, appliqué stitch the Right and Left Claws onto the Crab Shell. Stitch along the back of the Claws only (opposite the pincher). Set aside.

3 > Mark the position of the snap closures on the Lining about ½" from the top and bottom edges, as shown. Sew the snap closures in place.

4 > Align the Crab Shell and Lining felt back to back, and pin them together. Blanket stitch them together, starting at the bottom right. When you reach the Right Claw, insert the Right Legs felt between the Shell and Lining pieces. Continue to blanket stitch through them to secure them in place. Repeat for the Left Legs when you reach the Left Claw. Continue blanket stitching all the way around.

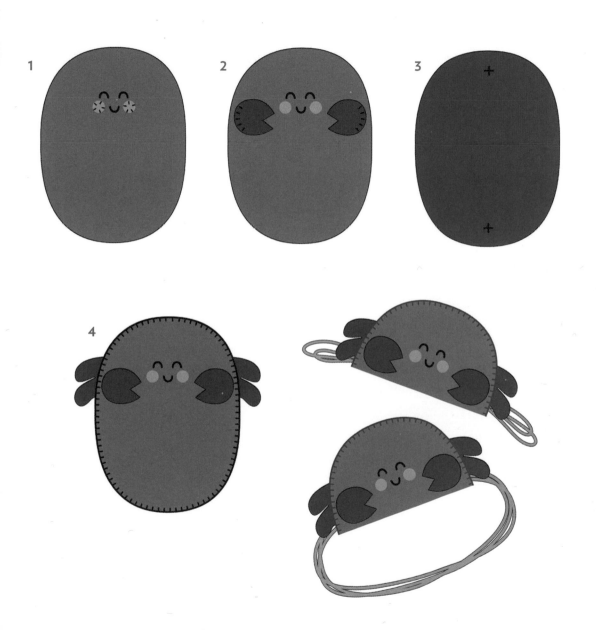

1

2

3

4

FUDGE POP PLUSHIE

There's nothing better than a fudge-dipped ice cream bar on a warm summer day. Unless, of course, it's an adorable Fudge Pop Plushie! A quick and fun project to stitch, this sweet plushie can feature your favorite choice of topping, with a dash of colorful bead sprinkles. Best of all, it won't melt—though it's sure to melt your heart!

Mix and match felt colors to create your own unique Fudge Pop flavors!

materials

- ✗ **Ice Cream: 4½" x 5" pink felt**

- ✗ **Embroidery floss in the following colors: pink, brown, white, black**

- ✗ **2 Cheeks: 1" x 2" pink felt**

- ✗ **Seed beads in various colors (about 50)**

- ✗ **Fudge: 5" x 5½" dark brown felt**

- ✗ **Stick: 2" x 2" beige felt**

- ✗ **Backing: 8" x 6" blue felt**

- ✗ **Poly-fill stuffing**

- ✗ **Scissors**

- ✗ **Straight pins**

- ✗ **Marking pen**

- ✗ **Embroidery needle**

Cut out the templates (page 166). Pin the templates to the felt pieces, and cut carefully along the lines. Once you've cut out all the felt pieces, you're ready to begin!

Use 3 strands of embroidery floss to stitch this project.

1 > Mark the Eyes and Mouth on the Ice Cream felt, using a marking pen. Use black thread to backstitch the face detail. Appliqué stitch the Cheeks in place with matching thread.

2 > Stitch bead "sprinkles" randomly onto the Fudge felt, using brown thread.

3 > Place the Fudge over the Ice Cream felt, overlapping by about ¼". Pin in place. Appliqué stitch the Fudge to the Ice Cream felt, using thread to match the Fudge.

4 > Place the Ice Cream over the Stick felt, overlapping by about ¼". Pin in place. Appliqué stitch the Ice Cream to the Stick felt, using thread to match the Ice Cream.

5 > Place the Fudge Pop atop the Backing felt and pin them together. Carefully cut along the edges until you have a perfectly matched backing piece. Do not remove the pins.

6 > Using a brightly colored thread, blanket stitch the Fudge Pop and Backing together, starting near the top left, removing the pins as you go. When you're about 2" away from where you started, begin gently stuffing with poly-fill (use a pencil or chopsticks if needed). Once the Fudge Pop has reached your desired poofiness, continue to blanket stitch shut.

1

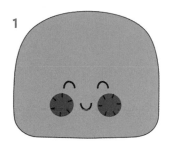

2

3

4

6

GIRAFFE WINE BOTTLE TOPPER

What's tall and towering and pairs perfectly with cheese and wine? This adorable giraffe wine bottle topper! Quick and easy to stitch, this project makes a fun and quirky gift for the wine lover in your life. Simply place it on your favorite wine bottle and achieve instant honored guest status when you go to your next dinner party. Or use it to add a touch of whimsy to your own wine rack at home.

materials

- ✕ **Front and Back Body: 7″ x 8″ rusty orange felt**
- ✕ **Embroidery floss in the following colors: rusty orange, black**
- ✕ **Muzzle: 2″ x 3″ cream felt**
- ✕ **2 Ears: 1″ x 2″ rusty orange felt**
- ✕ **Horns: 2″ x 2″ dark brown felt**
- ✕ **2 Cheeks: 1″ x 2″ pink felt**
- ✕ **Spots: 3″ x 4″ dark brown felt**
- ✕ **Scissors**
- ✕ **Straight pins**
- ✕ **Marking pen**
- ✕ **Embroidery needle**
- ✕ **Fabric glue**
- ✕ **Small paintbrush**

Cut out the templates (page 167). Pin the templates to the felt pieces, and cut carefully along the lines. Once you've cut out all the felt pieces, you're ready to begin!

Use 3 strands of embroidery floss to stitch this project.

1 > Mark the Eyes on the Front Body felt, using a marking pen. Use black thread to backstitch the eye detail.

2 > Mark the Nostrils on the Muzzle Felt. Use black thread to backstitch the nostril detail. Set aside.

3 > Align the Front and Back Body felt and pin them together. Blanket stitch them together with matching thread, starting at the lower right corner. When you are near the top right, insert the Right Ear between the Front and Back Body felt. Blanket stitch through to secure the Ear in place. Repeat for the Horns and the Left Ear. Continue to blanket stitch until you reach the lower left corner. Fasten off, leaving the bottom open.

4 > Glue the Muzzle onto the Front Body felt with fabric glue, as shown. Glue the Cheeks onto the Muzzle.

5 > Glue the Spots randomly onto the giraffe's neck on the Front Body felt.

LITTLE LLAMA ORNAMENT

Meet Llama. He's hip, he's cool—just the sort of buddy you want hanging around! From the tip of his cute little ears all the way down to his fuzzy feet, Llama's got charm to spare. Fun and easy to stitch, you'll want to create a small herd in bright and festive colors to decorate your abode.

materials

- 12″ length baker's twine
- Embroidery floss in the following colors: beige, pink, blue, black
- Llama Body: 5½″ x 4″ light brown felt
- Muzzle: 1″ x 1″ brown felt
- Nose: 1″ x 1″ dark brown felt
- 2 Cheeks: 1″ x 2″ pink felt
- Llama Backing: 5½″ x 4″ sky blue felt
- Blanket: 1½″ x 1½″ turquoise felt
- 2 Ears: 1″ x 1″ brown felt
- Poly-fill stuffing

- Scissors
- Straight pins
- Marking pen
- Fabric glue
- Small paintbrush
- Embroidery needle

Cut a 12" length of baker's twine and knot the ends together, making a large loop.

Cut out the templates (page 168). Pin the templates to the felt pieces, and cut carefully along the lines. Once you've cut out all the felt pieces, you're ready to begin!

Use 3 strands of embroidery floss to stitch this project.

1 › Mark the Eyes on the Llama Body felt with a marking pen. Use black thread to backstitch the eye detail. Appliqué stitch the Muzzle felt in place with matching thread. Mark the Mouth on the Muzzle felt. Use black thread to backstitch the mouth detail. Glue the Nose above the mouth detail.

2 › Appliqué stitch the Cheeks in place with matching thread. With brightly colored thread, backstitch the Blanket in place along the bottom only.

3 › Align the Llama Body and Backing felt and pin them together. Using brightly colored thread, blanket stitch the two together, starting at the lower neck. When you've reached the tail, pause and gently stuff the legs with poly-fill.

4 › Continue to blanket stitch until you are almost at the top right corner of the head. Insert the Right Ear between the Llama Body and the Backing felt, and continue to blanket stitch through to secure it in place. When you reach the top center of the head, insert the twine (knot side down) between the Llama Body and the Backing felt. Continue to blanket stitch, making sure to catch the twine between stitches to secure it in place. Insert the Left Ear as you did with the Right Ear.

5 › When you are about 1" away from where you started, gently stuff the Llama with more poly-fill. Continue to blanket stitch shut.

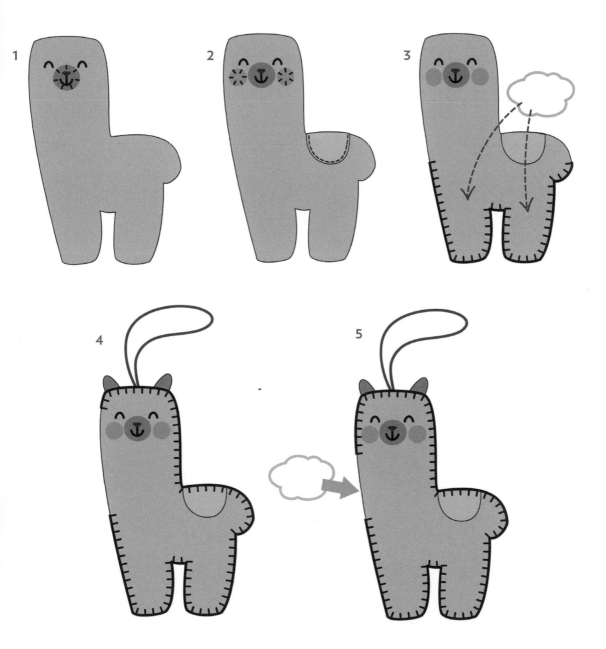

FROSTY TREAT CHARMS

Quite possibly the cutest little charms ever, this trio of frosty treats is sure to sweeten anything it adorns. They're petite and perfectly delightful to stitch, with lots of precious details. Attach these kawaii cuties to a bracelet, a necklace, zippers, or anywhere else! Choose your favorite frosty treat or stitch them all.

materials

- ✖ Embroidery floss in the following colors: white, pink, beige, mint, red, orange, green, blue, black
- ✖ 3 lobster clasp findings
- ✖ 3 metal jump rings
- ✖ Poly-fill stuffing
- ✖ Scissors
- ✖ Straight pins
- ✖ Marking pen
- ✖ Embroidery needle
- ✖ Fabric glue
- ✖ Small paintbrush

FUDGE POP

- ✖ Ice Cream: 2″ x 2″ yellow felt
- ✖ 2 Cheeks: 1″ x 2″ pink felt
- ✖ Fudge: 2″ x 2½″ pink felt
- ✖ Stick and Stick Backing: 1″ x 2″ beige felt
- ✖ Backing: 2½″ x 3″ sky blue felt
- ✖ 1″ yellow ribbon

ICE CREAM CONE

- ✖ Ice Cream: 2½″ x 2″ mint felt
- ✖ 2 Cheeks: 1″ x 2″ pink felt
- ✖ Cone: 2″ x 2″ light brown felt
- ✖ Backing: 3½″ x 2½″ pink felt
- ✖ 1″ light brown ribbon

ROCKET POP

- ✖ White: 1½″ x 2½″ white felt
- ✖ 2 Cheeks: 1″ x 2″ pink felt
- ✖ Stick and Stick Backing: 1″ x 2″ beige felt
- ✖ Red: 1″ x 2″ red felt
- ✖ Blue: 1″ x 2½″ blue felt
- ✖ Backing: 2½″ x 3″ sky blue felt
- ✖ 1″ red ribbon

Cut out the templates (page 169). Pin the templates to the felt pieces, and cut carefully along the lines. Once you've cut out all the felt pieces, you're ready to begin!

Use 3 strands of embroidery floss to stitch this project.

FUDGE POP

1 > Mark the Eyes and Mouth on the Ice Cream felt. Use black thread to backstitch the face detail. Glue the Cheeks in place with fabric glue.

2 > Stitch "sprinkles" onto the Fudge felt, using various colors of thread.

3 > Glue the Stick Front and Stick Backing felt pieces together. Set aside.

4 > Glue the Fudge onto the top half of the Ice Cream felt, overlapping by about ¼".

5 > Place the Fudge Pop atop the Backing felt and pin them together. Carefully cut along the edges until you have a perfectly matched backing piece. Using matching thread, whipstitch the Fudge Pop and Backing felt together, starting in the middle on the right.

6 > Just before you reach the top center, fold the ribbon in half and insert the ribbon (cut edges down) between the Fudge Pop and the Backing felt, leaving about ¼" of ribbon as a loop. Carefully stitch through the ribbon to secure it in place.

7 > Continue to whipstitch until you reach the bottom center. Insert the Stick between the Fudge Pop and the Backing, and stitch through to secure the Stick in place. When you're about 1" from where you started, gently stuff the Fudge Pop with poly-fill and whipstitch shut. Insert the jump ring into the ribbon loop. Attach the lobster clasp finding to the jump ring.

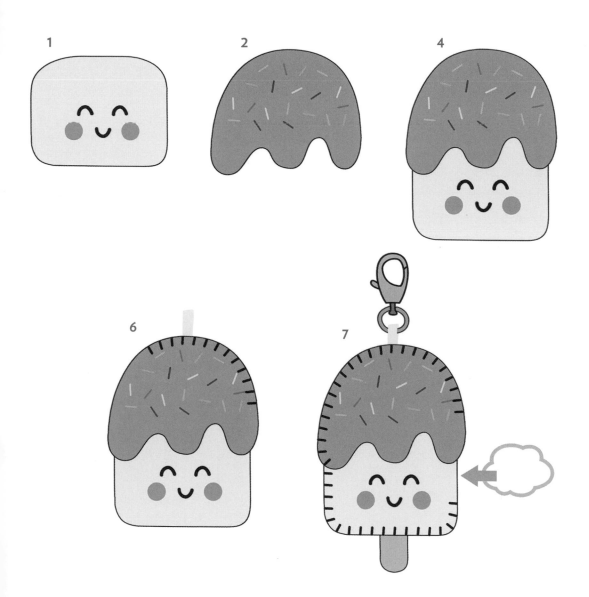

ICE CREAM CONE

1 〉 Mark the Eyes and Mouth on the Ice Cream felt, using a marking pen. Use black thread to backstitch the face detail. Glue the Cheeks in place.

2 〉 Mark the cone detail on the Cone felt. Backstitch the cone detail with matching thread.

3 〉 Glue the Ice Cream onto the top portion of the Cone felt, overlapping by about ¼".

4 〉 Place the Ice Cream Cone atop the Backing felt and pin them together. Carefully cut along the edges until you have a perfectly matched backing piece. Using matching thread, whipstitch the Ice Cream Cone and the Backing felt together, starting at the middle on the right.

5 〉 Just before you reach the top center, fold the ribbon in half and insert the ribbon (cut edges down) between the Ice Cream Cone and the Backing felt, leaving about ¼" of ribbon as a loop. Carefully stitch through the ribbon to secure it in place.

6 〉 Continue to whipstitch around until you are about 1" from where you started. Gently stuff the Ice Cream Cone with poly-fill and whipstitch shut. Insert a jump ring into the ribbon loop. Attach the lobster clasp finding to the jump ring.

ROCKET POP

1 > Mark the Eyes and Mouth on the White felt. Use black thread to backstitch the face detail. Glue the Cheeks in place with fabric glue.

2 > Glue the Stick Front and Stick Back felt pieces together. Set aside.

3 > Glue the Red felt atop the White felt, as shown. Glue the White felt atop the Blue felt as shown.

4 > Place the Rocket Pop atop the Backing felt and pin them together. Carefully cut along the edges until you have a perfectly matched backing piece. Using matching thread, whipstitch the Rocket Pop and the Backing felt together, starting at the middle on the right.

5 > Just before reaching the top center, fold the ribbon in half and insert the ribbon (cut edges down) between the Rocket Pop and the Backing felt, leaving about ¼" of ribbon as a loop. Carefully stitch through the ribbon to secure it in place.

6 > Continue to whipstitch until you reach the bottom center. Insert the Stick between the Rocket Pop and the Backing. Stitch through it to secure it in place. When you're about 1" from where you started, gently stuff the Rocket Pop with poly-fill and whipstitch it shut. Insert a jump ring into the ribbon loop. Attach the lobster clasp finding to the jump ring.

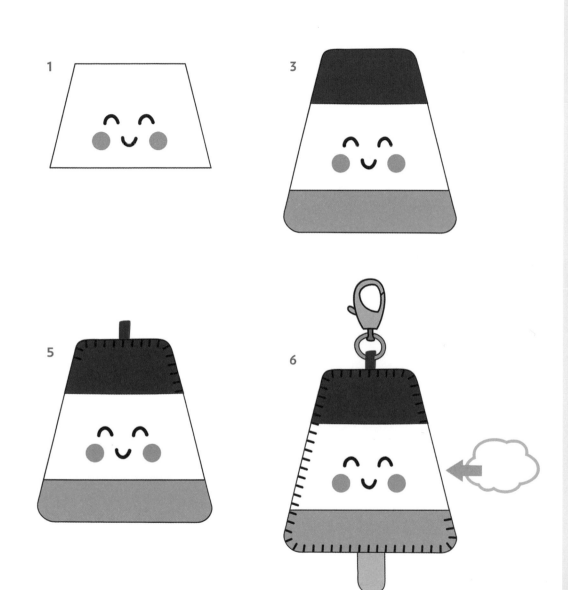

SWEET SLOTH PENCIL TOPPER

Though not the most active critter in the animal kingdom, this sweet sloth has other redeeming qualities, and his tranquil disposition makes him the ideal office mate. You'll love his serene expression as he hangs onto your pencil, reminding you that it's good to pause and just enjoy the moment. A quick project to stitch, you may be tempted to make more than one!

materials

✕ **Embroidery floss in the following colors:** white, beige, black

✕ **Face:** 1½″ x 1½″ white felt

✕ **Front and Back Body:** 3″ x 4″ brown felt

✕ **2 Cheeks:** 1″ x 2″ pink felt

✕ **Left and Right Mask:** 1″ x 1″ light brown felt

✕ **Nose:** 1″ x 1″ brown felt

✕ **Arm:** 1″ x 2″ brown felt

✕ **Pencil Holder:** 2″ x 1½″ brown felt

✕ **Scissors**

✕ **Straight pins**

✕ **Marking pen**

✕ **Embroidery needle**

✕ **Fabric glue**

✕ **Small paintbrush**

Cut out the templates (page 170). Pin the templates to the felt pieces, and cut carefully along the lines. Once you've cut out all the felt pieces, you're ready to begin!

Use 3 strands of embroidery floss to stitch this project.

1 > Mark the Mouth on the Face felt with a marking pen. Use black thread to backstitch the mouth detail. Appliqué stitch the Face onto the Front Body felt, as shown. Glue the Cheeks in place with fabric glue.

2 > Mark the Eyes on the Left and Right Mask felt. Use black thread to backstitch the eye detail. Glue the Left and Right Mask onto the Face felt. Glue the Nose in place.

3 > Mark the Claws on the Front Body felt with a marking pen. Use beige thread to backstitch the claw detail.

4 > Mark the Claws on the Arm felt. Use light-colored thread to backstitch the claw detail. Glue the Arm onto the Front Body felt, as shown.

5 > Fold the Pencil Holder felt in half lengthwise, and glue the ends together only.

6 > Align the Front and Back Body felt and glue them together. Glue the Pencil Holder felt to the Back Body felt, as shown. Let it dry completely before using, about 20 minutes.

DOUGHNUT COASTER

Fun meets function with these delightful doughnut coasters. Pick your favorite frosting flavor, add some colorful "sprinkles," and you're all set. Your guests will love these sugary doughnuts' cheerful smiles, and you'll love how well they protect your tabletop. Don't be surprised if you're charmed into stitching a baker's dozen!

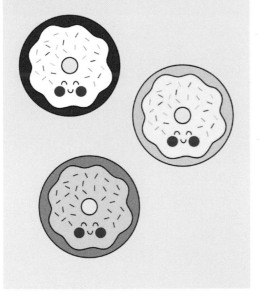

Mix and match felt colors to create your own unique doughnut coaster flavors!

Cut out the templates (page 170). Pin the templates to the felt pieces, and cut carefully along the lines. Once you've cut out all the felt pieces, you're ready to begin!

Use 3 strands of embroidery floss to stitch this project.

1 > Place the Frosting onto the Doughnut Top, and pin it in place. Appliqué stitch the Frosting along the outer edge only, using thread to match the Frosting.

2 > Mark the Eyes and Mouth on the Frosting felt with a marking pen. Use black thread to backstitch the face detail. (Make your stitches small to ensure smooth curves.) Appliqué stitch the Cheeks in place with matching thread or glue them in place with fabric glue.

3 > Stitch "sprinkles" onto the Frosting, using various colors of thread.

4 > Align the Doughnut Bottom with the Doughnut Top, and pin them together. With matching thread, whipstitch the two pieces together around the edge of the doughnut.

5 > Using thread to match the Frosting, whipstitch the Frosting, the Doughnut Top, and the Doughnut Bottom together around the center hole.

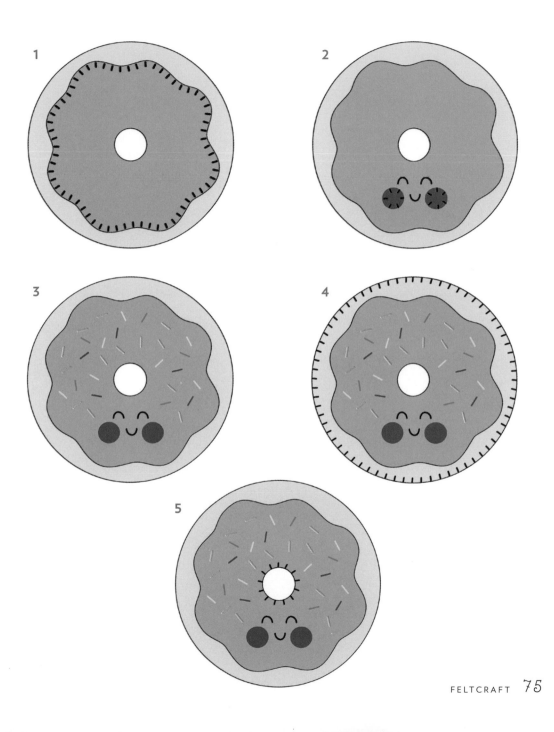

WOODLAND CRITTERS GARLAND

Owl, Hedgehog, and Fox are three dear friends who love to hang together. Their serene expressions and precious stitchwork evoke a sense of rustic woodland whimsy. They are simple and calming to stitch, and would look oh so cute strung across the mantel, the bookcase, the headboard, a tree, or anyplace at all. And if you're feeling really adventurous, how about stitching more than one of each critter?

materials

- ✗ Embroidery floss in the following colors: gray, dark gray, beige, cream, rusty orange, white, dark brown, black
- ✗ Poly-fill stuffing
- ✗ 36″ length baker's twine
- ✗ Scissors
- ✗ Straight pins
- ✗ Embroidery needle
- ✗ Marking pen
- ✗ Fabric glue
- ✗ Small paintbrush

OWL

- ✗ Chest: 2½″ x 3″ white felt
- ✗ Front and Back Body: 7″ x 3½″ gray felt
- ✗ 2 Cheeks: 1″ x 2″ pink felt
- ✗ Beak: 1″ x 1″ orange felt
- ✗ Right and Left Wings: 2″ x 2″ dark gray felt
- ✗ Small Rectangle: 1″ x 1″ gray felt
- ✗ Left and Right Feet: 1″ x 2″ orange felt

FOX

- ✗ Chest: 2½″ x 3″ cream felt
- ✗ Front and Back Body: 7″ x 3½″ rusty orange felt
- ✗ 2 Cheeks: 1″ x 2″ pink felt
- ✗ Nose: 1″ x 1″ dark brown felt
- ✗ Tail Tip: 1½″ x 1½″ white felt
- ✗ Tail: 2″ x 2½″ rusty orange felt
- ✗ Left and Right Legs: 2″ x 3″ dark brown felt
- ✗ Small Rectangle: 1″ x 1″ rusty orange felt
- ✗ Left and Right Ears: 1″ x 2″ dark brown felt

HEDGEHOG

- × **Front and Back Body:** 7″x 3½″ dark brown felt

- × **Chest:** 3″x 3″ cream felt

- × **Ears, Paws, Feet:** 2″x 3″ light brown felt

- × **2 Cheeks:** 1″x 2″ pink felt

- × **Nose:** 1″x 1″ dark brown felt

- × **Small Rectangle:** 1″x 1″ dark brown felt

Cut out the templates (pages 171–173). Pin the templates to the felt pieces, and cut carefully along the lines. Once you've cut out all the felt pieces, you're ready to begin!

Use 3 strands of embroidery floss to stitch this project.

OWL

1 > Appliqué stitch the Chest onto the Front Body felt. Mark the Eyes and the feather detail on the Chest felt with a marking pen. Use black thread to backstitch the eye and feather detail. Glue the Cheeks and Beak in place.

2 > Position the Right Wing onto the Front Body felt and, with matching thread, appliqué stitch it in place along the top only. Repeat for the Left Wing.

3 > Position the Small Rectangle near the top of the Back Body felt. Appliqué stitch it in place along the top and bottom only.

4 > Align the Front and Back Body felt and pin them together. Blanket stitch them together, starting at the upper right. (Do not stitch through the wings.) When you reach the lower left, insert the Left Foot between the Front and Back Body felt. Continue to stitch through to secure the foot in place. Repeat for the Right Foot.

5 > Continue to stitch until you are about 1″ from where you started. Gently stuff with poly-fill and stitch shut.

FOX

1 > With matching thread, appliqué stitch the Chest onto the Front Body felt. Mark the Eyes on the Chest felt, using a marking pen. Use black thread to back-stitch the eye detail. Glue the Cheeks and Nose in place.

2 > Glue the Tail Tip to the Tail felt, as shown. Set aside.

3 > With matching thread, appliqué stitch the Right Leg to the Chest felt along the top only. Repeat for the Left Leg.

4 > Position the Small Rectangle near the top of the Back Body felt. Appliqué stitch it in place along the top and bottom only.

5 > Align the Front and Back Body felt, and pin them together. Starting at the bottom left corner, blanket stitch the bottom together until you reach the bottom right corner. (Do not stitch through the Legs.) Insert the Tail between the Front and Back Body felt, as shown.

6 > Continue to blanket stitch until you reach the top right corner. Insert the Right Ear between the Front and Back Body felt. Continue stitching through to secure the Ear in place. When you get to the top left, repeat for the Left Ear.

7 > Continue to stitch until you are about 1″ from where you started. Gently stuff with poly-fill and stitch shut.

HEDGEHOG

1 > With matching thread, appliqué stitch the Chest felt onto the Front Body felt, starting at the bottom right corner. When you reach the top right, insert the Right Ear between the Chest felt and the Front Body felt. Continue stitching through to secure the Right Ear in place. When you get to the top left, repeat for the Left Ear. Continue stitching the Chest to the Front Body and stop when you reach the bottom left corner. (Leave the bottom unstitched.)

2 > Mark the Eyes on the Chest felt, using a marking pen. Use black thread to back-stitch the eye detail. Glue the Cheeks and Nose in place with fabric glue. Appliqué stitch the Paws in place below the Cheeks, as shown, stitching along the top only. Appliqué stitch the Feet in place, as shown, stitching along the top only.

3 > Using cream-colored thread, make random single-stitch spines around the Front Body felt.

4 > Position the Small Rectangle near the top of the Back Body felt. Appliqué stitch it in place along the top and bottom only.

5 > Align the Front and Back Body felt and pin them together. Starting at the mid-right, blanket stitch them together until you are about 1" from where you started. (Do not stitch through the feet.) Gently stuff with poly-fill and stitch shut.

Finishing Touch
Once your woodland critter trio is stitched, thread a jumbo tapestry needle with a 36" length of twine and insert it through the Small Rectangle on the back of each critter so you can hang them as a garland.

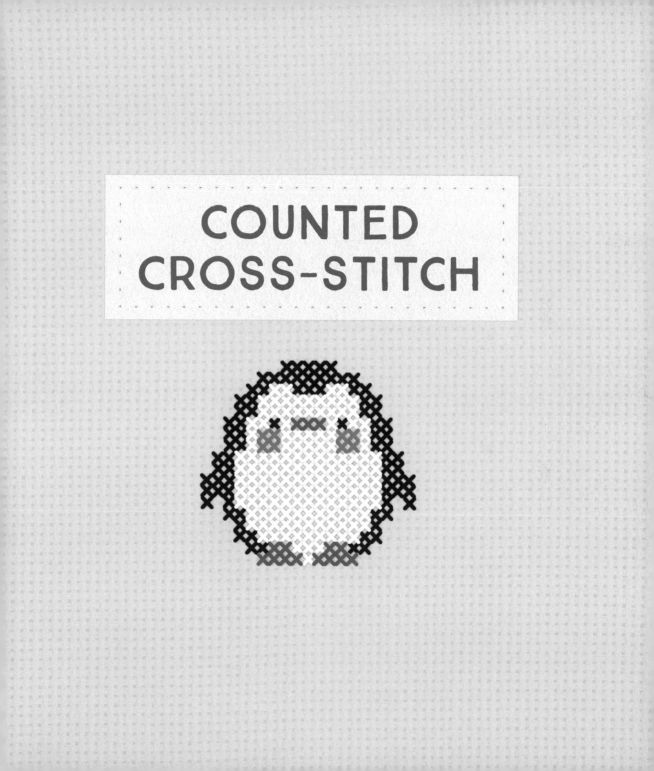

COUNTED CROSS-STITCH

CUTE ANIMALS WINEGLASS CHARMS

We think these cute wineglass charms have a somewhat sophisticated dinner party animal vibe to them. Stitched on plastic aida, they're sure to make adorable conversation pieces. Your guests will delight in choosing their favorite friend: Tabby Cat, Frog, Bunny, or Panda. You'll definitely want to create a set or two for your next get-together.

materials

× **Four 2″ x 2″ squares of 14-count plastic aida**

× **1 skein each of the embroidery floss colors in the design chart**

× **Four 2″ x 2″ squares of white felt**

× **4 wine charm rings**

× **4 jump rings**

× **Tapestry needle**

× **Scissors**

× **Fabric glue**

× **Small paintbrush**

× **Straight pin**

× **Small pliers**

Use 2 strands of embroidery floss for this project.

1 〉 Cross-stitch each design onto an aida square.

2 〉 When you're finished stitching the design, use sharp scissors to carefully cut the excess aida one full square away from the design's edge on all sides.

3 〉 Using a small paintbrush, gently apply fabric glue to the stitches on the back of the charm. (Be careful not to use too much glue or it will come through the holes to the right side.) Place the charm (glue side down) onto the center of the 2″ x 2″ square of white felt. Gently press down. Let dry for at least 2 hours.

4 〉 Once the glue has dried completely, carefully cut the excess felt by following the edge of the aida.

5 〉 Using a sharp pin, poke a hole through the aida and felt at the place where you wish to insert the jump ring. Open the jump ring with the pliers and insert it carefully through the hole. Close the jump ring. Add the wine charm ring to the jump ring.

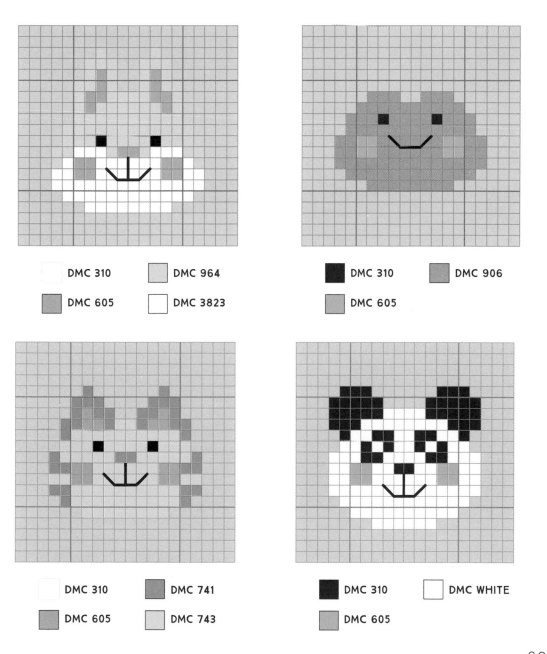

DMC 310   DMC 964

DMC 605   DMC 3823

DMC 310   DMC 906

DMC 605

DMC 310   DMC 741

DMC 605   DMC 743

DMC 310   DMC WHITE

DMC 605

HAPPY AVOCADO GIFT TAG

Why is the avocado such a popular fruit? (And yes, it's a fruit, not a vegetable!) We like to think it's because of that sweet smile, those bright pink cheeks, and that mellow personality. Or maybe it's the way the cross-stitches bring this happy little guy to life. Tie this adorable tag to gifts, gift bags, flowers, mason jars, or anything that needs a touch of avocado charm, and you'll instantly bring joy to someone special.

materials:

✗ **1 skein each of the embroidery floss colors in the design chart**

✗ **One 5½" x 5½" piece of 14-count white cloth aida**

✗ **Double-sided craft tape**

✗ **12" length baker's twine**

✗ **Scissors**

✗ **Tapestry needle**

✗ **Standard ¼" hole punch**

Print and cut out the gift tag template (page 174).

Use 2 strands of embroidery floss for this project.

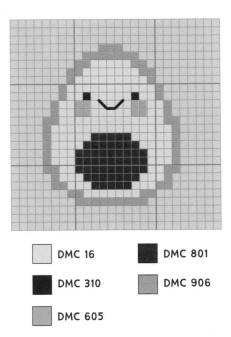

1 〉 Cross-stitch the design onto the aida square.

2 〉 When you're finished stitching the design, use sharp scissors to carefully cut the excess aida four full squares away from the design's edge, on all sides.

3 〉 Fray the two outermost squares by gently pulling the aida thread outward, starting at the corners.

4 〉 Center and adhere the aida to the gift tag with strong double-sided craft tape. Punch a hole on top of the gift tag and insert a 12″ length of baker's twine.

DMC 16   DMC 801

DMC 310   DMC 906

DMC 605

"I'M HOT FOR YOU" GREETING CARD

Sometimes you just have to say what you feel. Or, in this case, let this adorable little cross-stitch do the talking for you! This project features a too-cute, spicy-red pepper, playful lettering, and bright colors. Just clip the design when finished and tape it to a pretty blank card for gifting. But beware: It makes a bold and flirty statement!

materials

- × 1 skein each of the embroidery floss colors in the design chart
- × One 7″ x 7″ square of 14-count white cloth aida
- × Blank A2 (4¼″ x 5½″) greeting card
- × Double-sided craft tape
- × Tapestry needle
- × Scissors

Use 2 strands of embroidery floss for this project.

1 〉 Cross-stitch the design onto the aida.

2 〉 When you're finished stitching the design, use sharp scissors to carefully cut the excess aida five full squares away from the design's edge, on all sides.

3 〉 Fray the outermost squares by gently pulling the aida thread outwards, starting at the corners.

4 〉 Center and affix the aida to the front of the greeting card with strong double-sided craft tape.

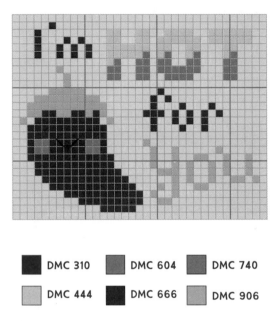

DMC 310 DMC 604 DMC 740

DMC 444 DMC 666 DMC 906

CACTUS GARDEN SMARTPHONE CASE

Keeping your smartphone safe and scratch-free has never been so stylish. Cactus gardens are all the rage, and this kawaii trio is dedicated to being hip and trendy. This project is fun and functional, with bright blanket stitch edging and a pretty running stitch detail securing the cross-stitch design to the felt sleeve. Have fun with felt colors and don't be surprised if your friends want one, too!

materials:

- **✗ One 7½" x 5½" piece of 14-count white cloth aida**
- **✗ 9" x 12" sheet of green felt**
- **✗ 1 skein each of the embroidery floss colors in the design chart**
- **✗ Tapestry needle**
- **✗ Embroidery needle**
- **✗ Scissors**
- **✗ Straight pins**

Use 2 strands of embroidery floss for the cross-stitch portion of this project. Use 3 strands for all other stitching.

1 > To make the felt smartphone case, you will first need to make a custom smartphone template. Make one by tracing your phone onto a piece of paper. Measure and mark ½" out from all sides, then connect the markings to create your custom template. (Use the corners of your phone to round off the corners of the template.)

2 > Use this template to cut two matching pieces of green felt, one for the Front and one for the Back of the smartphone case.

3 > Cross-stitch the cactus garden design onto the aida.

4 > When you're finished stitching the design, use sharp scissors to carefully cut the excess aida five full squares away from the design's edge, on all sides.

5 > Fray the outermost squares by gently pulling the aida thread outwards, starting at the corners.

6 > Center the aida on the Front felt and pin it in place. Secure it in place with a running stitch in a brightly colored thread.

7 > Align the Front and Back felt pieces and pin them together. With a brightly colored thread, blanket stitch the two together along the sides and bottom, leaving one short side open for inserting your phone.

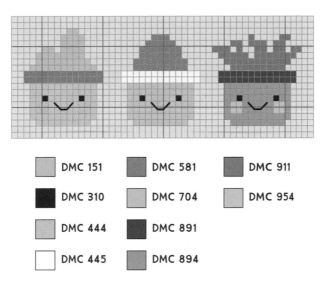

DMC 151	DMC 581	DMC 911
DMC 310	DMC 704	DMC 954
DMC 444	DMC 891	
DMC 445	DMC 894	

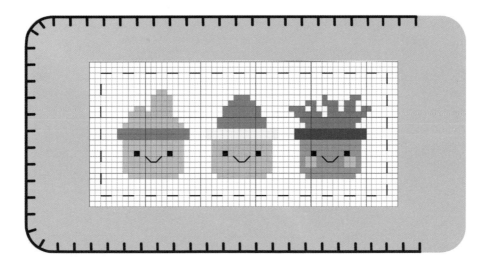

SEAL AND PENGUIN CUPCAKE TOPPERS

Did you know that Seal and Penguin are the original party animals? This adorable duo is a cool addition to any party! They feel right at home atop frosted cupcakes and iced sugar glazes, and they love a snowy dusting of powdered sugar. Stitched on plastic aida, Seal and Penguin are reusable, which also makes them the perfect little party favor.

materials

- ✕ 1 skein each of the embroidery floss colors in the design chart
- ✕ Two 2½" x 2½" squares of 14-count plastic aida
- ✕ Two 2½" x 2½" squares of white felt
- ✕ One 2" x 2" piece of white felt
- ✕ 2 large toothpicks
- ✕ Tapestry needle
- ✕ Scissors
- ✕ Fabric glue
- ✕ Small paintbrush

Use 2 strands of embroidery floss for this project.

1 〉 Cross-stitch each design onto an aida square.

2 〉 Use sharp scissors to carefully cut the excess aida one full square away from the design's edge.

3 〉 Using a small paintbrush, gently apply fabric glue to the stitches on the back of the design. (Be careful not to use too much glue or it will come through the holes to the right side.) Place the design (glue side down) onto the center of the 2½″ x 2½″ square of white felt. Gently press down. Let it dry for at least 2 hours.

4 〉 Once the glue has dried completely, carefully cut the excess felt by following the edge of the aida.

5 〉 Using the template (page 174), cut a small rectangle out of white felt. Position the rectangle across the center of the back of the cupcake topper. Glue it down along the left and right sides only, leaving the center unglued for inserting the toothpick.

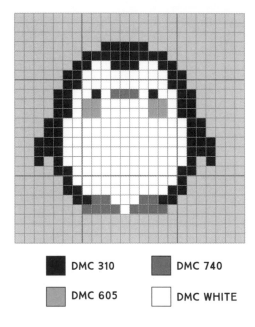

	DMC 310		DMC 740
	DMC 605		DMC WHITE

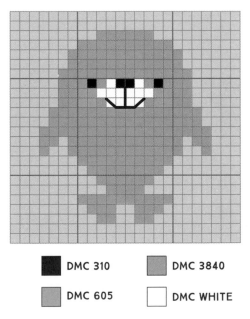

	DMC 310		DMC 3840
	DMC 605		DMC WHITE

TOADSTOOL AND ACORN NAPKIN RINGS

Whether you're having an al fresco lunch or setting a festive dinner table, these fun and quirky napkin rings will delight your guests. Toadstool and Acorn are naturally charming, with their earthy colors and soft felt rings. They're also super-easy to make, so you'll definitely want to stitch up a set for your next gathering.

materials

- ✖ **1 skein each of the embroidery floss colors in the design chart**
- ✖ **Two 2″ x 2″ squares of 14-count white cloth aida**
- ✖ **Napkin Ring: 8″ x 2″ green felt**
- ✖ **Napkin Ring: 8″ x 2″ brown felt**
- ✖ **Scissors**
- ✖ **Tapestry needle**
- ✖ **Fabric glue**
- ✖ **Small paintbrush**

Cut out 2 napkin ring templates (page 175). Pin the templates to the felt pieces, and cut carefully along the lines. Once you've cut out the felt pieces, you're ready to begin!

Use 2 strands of embroidery floss to stitch this project.

1 ⟩ Cross-stitch each design onto an aida square.

2 ⟩ When you're finished cross-stitching the designs, use sharp scissors to carefully cut the excess aida one full square away from each design's edge.

3 ⟩ Glue the design to the center of the Napkin Ring felt with a small paintbrush. Let it dry completely, about 20 minutes.

4 ⟩ Overlap the ends of the Napkin Ring felt by ½" and appliqué stitch the ends together.

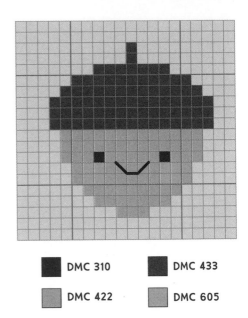

■ DMC 310   ■ DMC 433
■ DMC 422   ■ DMC 605

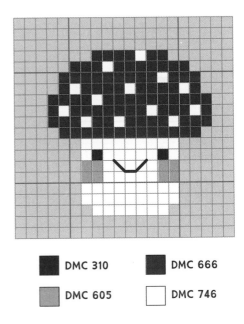

■ DMC 310   ■ DMC 666
■ DMC 605   ☐ DMC 746

LUCKY ELEPHANT MINI GIFT BAG

Elephants are legendary for bringing good luck, and the recipient of this adorable little gift bag will be lucky indeed! The front features a precious, geranium-pink, cross-stitched elephant. The felt gift bag is quick to stitch and adorned with dainty handles and button details. It's perfect for holding small treats or even jewelry.

materials

×   1 skein each of the embroidery floss colors in the design chart

×   7" x 7" square of 14-count white cloth aida

×   Gift Bag: 9½" x 5" turquoise felt

×   Handles (cut 2): 7½" x 1½" pink felt

×   4 colorful ½" buttons

×   Scissors

×   Straight pins

×   Tapestry needle

×   Embroidery needle

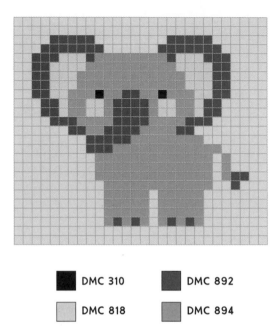

Cut out the templates (page 174). Pin the templates to the felt pieces, and cut carefully along the lines. Once you've cut out all the felt pieces, you're ready to begin!

Use 2 strands of embroidery floss for the cross-stitch portion of this project. Use 3 strands for all other stitching.

■ DMC 310	■ DMC 892
□ DMC 818	■ DMC 894

1 〉 Cross-stitch the design onto the aida.

2 〉 When you're finished stitching the design, use sharp scissors to carefully cut the excess aida five full squares away from the design's edge, on all sides.

3 〉 Fray the outermost squares by gently pulling the aida thread outwards, starting at the corners.

4 〉 Center the aida on the top-middle of the Gift Bag felt and pin it in place. Secure it with a running stitch.

5 〉 Fold the Gift Bag felt in half (with the cross-stitch facing out) and pin the edges together. With brightly colored thread, blanket stitch the edges.

6 〉 Attach the Handle to the top edge of the Gift Bag by sewing on two buttons, as shown. Repeat for second handle.

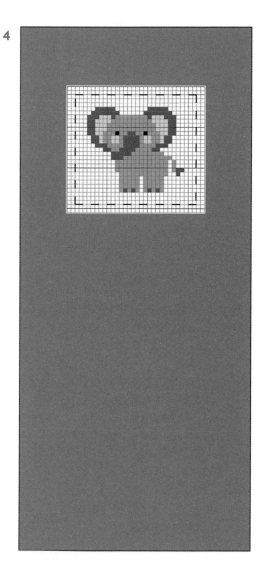

6

SUPER SUSHI MAGNETS

This stylish little sushi trio is too adorable to eat. But why not display them on your fridge? Cross-stitched on plastic aida, with a magnet detail, they're perfect for holding a photo, a shopping list, or a meal-plan chart. Or maybe they'll just be a cute little reminder that the sushi bar is what's for dinner.

materials

- ✗ **1 skein each of the embroidery floss colors in the design chart**

- ✗ **Two 2½" x 2" pieces and one 2" x 2" piece of 14-count plastic aida**

- ✗ **Two 2½" x 2" pieces and one 2" x 2" piece of white felt**

- ✗ **Three ½"-diameter flat, round magnets**

- ✗ **Tapestry needle**

- ✗ **Scissors**

- ✗ **Fabric glue**

- ✗ **Small paintbrush**

Use 2 strands of embroidery floss for this project.

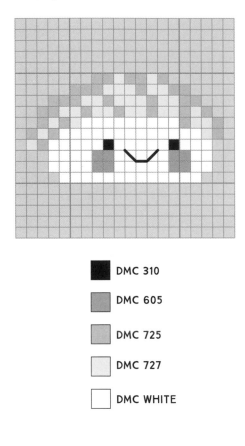

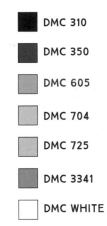

DMC 310

DMC 605

DMC 725

DMC 727

DMC WHITE

DMC 310

DMC 350

DMC 605

DMC 704

DMC 725

DMC 3341

DMC WHITE

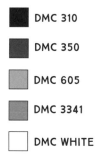 DMC 310

DMC 350

DMC 605

DMC 3341

DMC WHITE

1 › Cross-stitch each design onto an aida square.

2 › Use sharp scissors to carefully cut the excess aida one full square away from each design's edge.

3 › Using a small paintbrush, gently apply fabric glue to the stitches on the back of each design. (Be careful not to use too much glue or it will come through the holes to the right side.) Place each design (glue side down) onto the center of a piece of white felt. Gently press down. Let it dry for at least 2 hours.

4 › Once the glue has dried completely, carefully cut the excess felt by following the edge of the aida.

5 › Glue a small magnet onto the back of each sushi piece. Let it dry completely before using, about 20 minutes.

MILK AND COOKIE EARRINGS

Nothing says, "I'm crafty but sweet" better than this darling pair of milk and cookie earrings! This quick project is stitched on plastic aida with soft felt backing, making it light and oh so adorable. You may even be tempted to make a few as gifts!

materials

- ✕ Two 2″ x 2″ squares of 14-count plastic aida
- ✕ Two 2″ x 2″ squares of white felt
- ✕ 2 earring findings
- ✕ 2 jump rings
- ✕ 1 skein each of the embroidery floss colors in the design chart
- ✕ Tapestry needle
- ✕ Scissors
- ✕ Fabric glue
- ✕ Small paintbrush
- ✕ Sharp pin
- ✕ Small pliers

*Use 2 strands of embroidery floss for
this project.*

1 > Cross-stitch each design onto an
aida square.

2 > When you're finished cross-stitching the
design, use sharp scissors to carefully
cut the excess aida one full square away
from the design's edge.

3 > Using a small paintbrush, gently apply
fabric glue to the stitches on the back of
the charms. (Be careful not to use too
much glue or it will come through the
holes to the right side.) Place the charm
(glue side down) onto the center of the
2″ x 2″ square of white felt. Gently press
down. Let it dry for at least 2 hours.

4 > Once the glue has dried completely,
carefully cut the excess felt by following
the edge of the aida.

5 > Using a sharp pin, poke a hole through
the aida and felt at the place where you
wish to insert the jump ring. Open the
jump ring with the pliers and insert the
jump ring carefully through the hole.
Insert the earring finding into the jump
ring and close with the pliers.

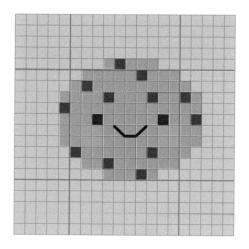

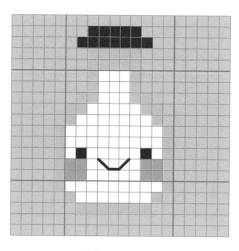

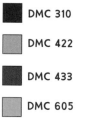 DMC 310

DMC 422

DMC 433

DMC 605

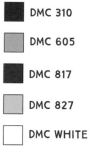 DMC 310

DMC 605

DMC 817

DMC 827

DMC WHITE

EMBROIDERY

CHEERFUL BLOOMS COIN PURSE

This lovely little coin purse is the height of sophistication. Featuring two cheerful blooms, a bright blanket stitch edging, and complementary lining, it's not only pretty but also functional. The easy-sew snap closure means loose change will not fall out and its size makes it perfect for holding makeup essentials, too.

materials

- **Purse Front: 5″ x 6″ bright yellow felt**
- **1 skein each of the embroidery floss colors in the design chart**
- **Purse Lining: 6½″ x 6″ pink felt**
- **Small snap closure (in 2 parts)**
- **Purse Back: 6½″ x 6″ dark yellow felt**
- **Scissors**
- **Straight pins**
- **Embroidery needle**
- **Marking pen**

■	DMC 310
■	DMC 3845
■	DMC 891
■	DMC 894
■	DMC 3609
■	DMC 946
■	DMC 704

Cut out the templates (page 175). Pin the templates to the felt pieces, and cut carefully along the lines. Once you've cut out all the felt pieces, you're ready to begin!

Use 3 strands of embroidery floss to stitch this project.

1 ⟩ Transfer the Blooms design onto the Purse Front felt, using your favorite transfer method (page 9).

2 ⟩ Backstitch the designs following the chart above.

3 ⟩ Mark the positions of the snap closures on the Purse Front and Lining felt with a marking pen, centered and about ½" from the top edge, as shown. Sew the snap closures in place.

4 ⟩ Align the Purse Front, Lining, and Purse Back. Pin them together. With brightly colored thread, blanket stitch all three layers together around the outer edge.

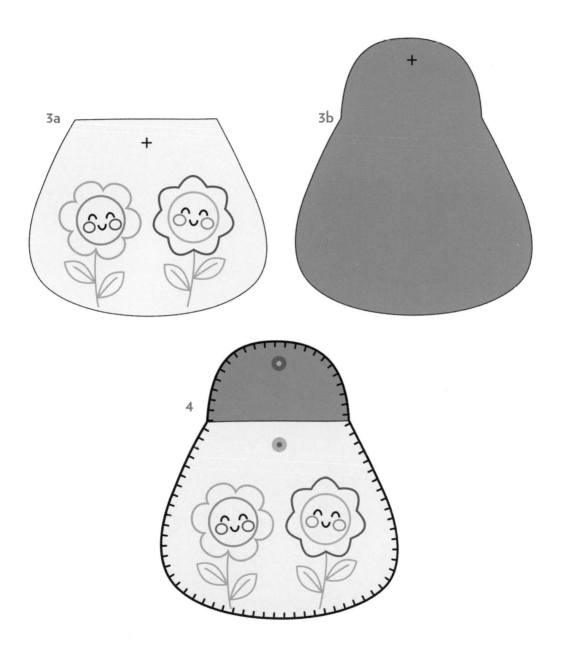

3a

3b

4

APPLE PIE APRON

What's more welcoming than a warm apple pie, fresh from the oven? Simple to stitch, this sweet apple pie has pretty steam details and a bright red pie pan. It's right at home on a classic chef's apron, something ruffled, or something vintage. And wouldn't it make a lovely gift for the baker in your life?

materials

✗ **Apron**

✗ **1 skein each of the embroidery floss colors in the design chart**

✗ **Embroidery needle**

✗ **Embroidery hoop**

✗ **Scissors**

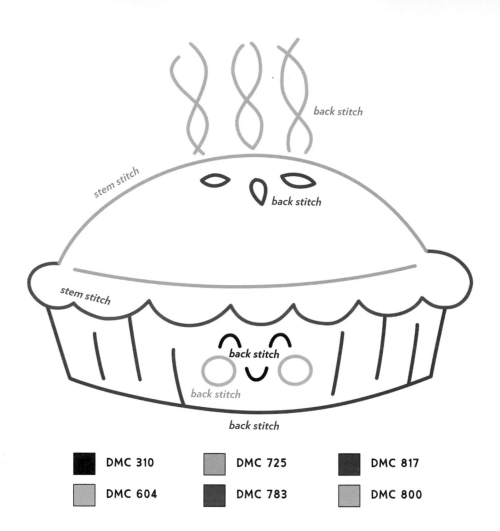

back stitch

stem stitch

back stitch

stem stitch

back stitch

back stitch

back stitch

■	DMC 310	■	DMC 725	■	DMC 817
■	DMC 604	■	DMC 783	■	DMC 800

Use 3 strands of floss to stitch this project.

1 > Transfer the Apple Pie design (page 176) onto the apron, using your favorite transfer method (page 9).

2 > Using an embroidery hoop, stitch the design following the chart above.

TIME FOR TEA TOWEL

It's always a good time for a cup of tea. This pretty little embroidered teacup and saucer will dress up your kitchen with its quaint kawaii charms. Stitch it on a crisp white flour-sack towel and drape it over the oven door handle for cozy kitchen vibes. It would make a great addition to the table linens at your next tea party, too.

materials

✖ **White flour-sack tea towel**

✖ **1 skein each of the embroidery floss colors in the design chart**

✖ **Embroidery needle**

✖ **Embroidery hoop**

✖ **Scissors**

■	DMC 310
■	DMC 3607
■	DMC 3806
■	DMC 783
■	DMC 3838
■	DMC 800
■	DMC 415
■	DMC 16

Use 3 strands of embroidery floss to stitch this project.

1 ⟩ Transfer the Teacup design (page 177) onto the bottom-center of the tea towel, using your favorite transfer method (page 9).

2 ⟩ Using an embroidery hoop, backstitch the design following the chart above.

TIP: When ironing your finished tea towel, avoid flattening your stitchwork by using the steam setting on the iron and gently pressing the back of the design.

LITTLE MONSTER ONESIE

Who doesn't love an adorable little monster, especially when he or she is sporting an equally adorable Little Monster onesie? This pudgy purple monster is too cute to cause any trouble, which makes him the perfect mascot for your little one. You'll love stitching his big silly feet and that toothy smile. And wouldn't he make the sweetest baby shower gift?

materials

×   Onesie

×   1 skein each of the embroidery floss colors in the design chart

×   Embroidery needle

×   Embroidery hoop

×   Scissors

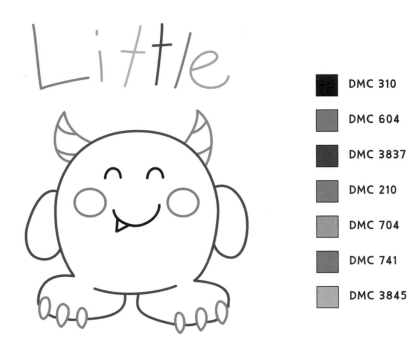

Little

■	DMC 310
■	DMC 604
■	DMC 3837
■	DMC 210
■	DMC 704
■	DMC 741
■	DMC 3845

TIPS: When using an embroidery hoop, keep it loose so you don't stretch the knit fabric. Keep your stitches about ¼″ long and try not to tug on them. (Tugging will pull the fabric and distort the design.) Gently iron or soak the onesie in warm water after stitching. Lay it flat to dry.

Use 3 strands of embroidery floss to stitch this project.

1 › Transfer the Little Monster design (page 180) onto the top-center of the onesie, using your favorite transfer method (page 9).

2 › Backstitch the design, following the chart above.

TRIP TO THE MARKET TOTE

A trip to the market doesn't have to be a chore, especially with this adorable embroidered market tote. Featuring a loaf of bread, farm-fresh eggs, a wedge of cheese, and a carton of milk, this charming design guarantees that you'll never forget the four staples! Whether you're a quick shopper or you like to browse, you'll love having these cheerful market buddies by your side.

materials

✕ **Canvas tote bag**

✕ **1 skein each of the embroidery floss colors in the design chart**

✕ **Embroidery needle**

✕ **Scissors**

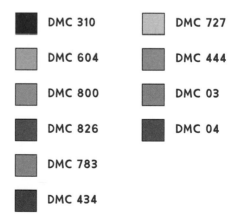

Use 3 strands of floss to stitch this project.

1 > Transfer the Market Tote designs (page 178) onto the center of the canvas tote using your favorite transfer method (page 9).

2 > Backstitch the designs following the chart above.

■ DMC 310	■ DMC 727
■ DMC 604	■ DMC 444
■ DMC 800	■ DMC 03
■ DMC 826	■ DMC 04
■ DMC 783	
■ DMC 434	

DRAGON BOOKMARK

Books and dragons just belong together, don't they? But, unlike dragons of yore, this cute little fire-breather is all about friendship. He'll happily hold the page for you with a classic ribbon bookmark. And you're sure to spot him peeking out the top as a sweet reminder to forget about the chores, make a cup of tea, and sit down with your favorite book.

materials

- 1 skein each of the embroidery floss colors in the design chart

- Front and Back: 4″ x 6″ moss green felt

- 10″ length ribbon

- Scissors

- Straight pins

- Embroidery needle

- Fabric glue

- Small paintbrush

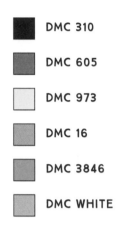

⬛	DMC 310
⬛	DMC 605
⬜	DMC 973
⬜	DMC 16
⬜	DMC 3846
⬜	DMC WHITE

Cut out the template (page 180). Pin the templates to the felt pieces, and cut carefully along the lines. Once you've cut out both felt pieces, you're ready to begin!

    Use 3 strands of floss to stitch this project.

1 ⟩ Transfer the Dragon design onto the Front felt, using your favorite transfer method (page 9).

2 ⟩ Backstitch the design following the chart above.

3 ⟩ Glue ½" of the ribbon to the bottom of the Back felt. Let it dry completely, about 20 minutes.

4 ⟩ Glue the Front and the Back felt together. Let it dry completely, about 20 minutes.

SWEET DREAMS SLUMBER MASK

With a silver moon and a bright shooting star, this slumber mask is too dreamy not to stitch! Embroidering on felt is always fun, and your stitches will really shine in this project. Choose a glittering elastic band for extra sparkle. A restful night's sleep is only a few blissful stitches away.

materials

- ✕ **Mask Front: 9″ x 4½″ charcoal gray felt**
- ✕ **1 skein each of the embroidery floss colors in the design chart**
- ✕ **Mask Lining: 9″ x 4½″ purple felt**
- ✕ **14″ elastic band**
- ✕ **Scissors**
- ✕ **Straight pins**
- ✕ **Embroidery needle**

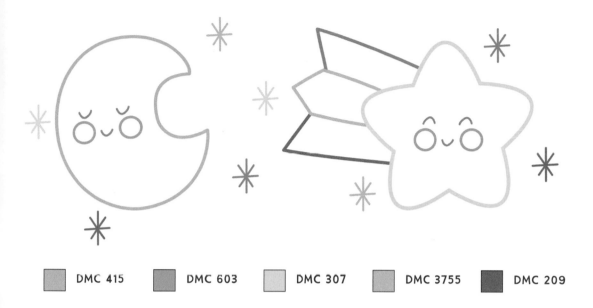

	DMC 415		DMC 603		DMC 307		DMC 3755		DMC 209

Cut out the templates (page 180). Pin the templates to the felt pieces, and cut carefully along the lines. Once you've cut out all the felt pieces, you're ready to begin!

Use 3 strands of embroidery floss to stitch this project.

1 〉 Transfer the Moon and Stars design onto the Mask Front felt, using your favorite transfer method (page 9).

2 〉 Backstitch the design following the chart above.

3 〉 Align the Mask Front and the Mask Lining felt, and pin them together, back to back. With matching thread, starting at the bottom center, sew the layers together with a blanket stitch along the outer edge. When you reach the right side, insert one end of the elastic band about ½" between the Mask Front and the Mask Lining felt. Continue to stitch through the elastic to secure in place. Repeat when you reach the left side. Stitch back to where you started and fasten off.

COFFEE SHOP TREATS CUP COZY

Everyone knows coffee's just an excuse to have a sweet treat. And what's better than fresh-baked muffins, gooey cinnamon rolls, or a big slice of chocolate cake? You can have them all with this adorable coffee shop cup cozy. It's an earth-friendly way to keep your hands cool while enjoying a hot cup of joe.

materials

- Cup Cozy: 11″ x 4″ mint felt
- 1 skein each of the embroidery floss colors in the design chart
- Lining: 11″ x 4″ pink felt
- Scissors
- Straight pins
- Embroidery needle

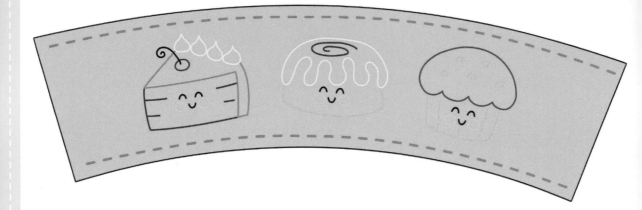

Cut out the templates (page 179). Pin the templates to the felt pieces, and cut carefully along the lines. Once you've cut out both felt pieces, you're ready to begin!

Use 3 strands of floss to stitch this project.

1 ⟩ Transfer the designs onto the Cup Cozy felt, using your favorite transfer method (page 9).

2 ⟩ Stitch the designs following the charts on page 145.

3 ⟩ Align the Cup Cozy and Lining felt, and pin them together, back to back. With brightly colored thread, sew the layers together with a running stitch along the top and bottom.

4 ⟩ Form the Cup Cozy into a ring and whipstitch the two ends together.

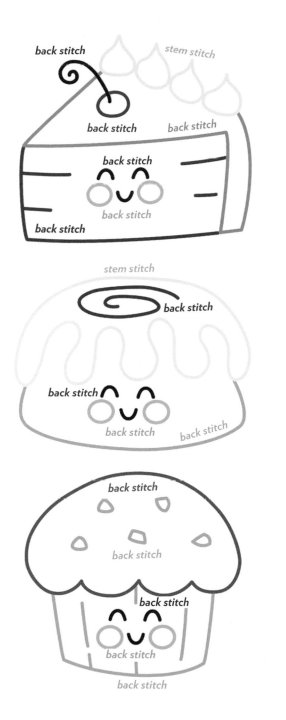

back stitch

stem stitch

back stitch

back stitch

back stitch

back stitch

back stitch

stem stitch

back stitch

back stitch

back stitch

back stitch

back stitch

back stitch

back stitch

back stitch

back stitch

■ DMC 310

■ DMC 605

■ DMC 3823

■ DMC 433

■ DMC 603

■ DMC 666

■ DMC 676

■ DMC 781

■ DMC 725

EAT YOUR VEGGIES NAPKINS

Eating your veggies was never so much fun! This darling napkin set features Leek, Turnip, Broccoli, and Carrot—four cheerful veggies to add a touch of kawaii garden charm to your next gathering. Embroider them on ultra-fine linen or soft cotton napkins, or give new life to vintage napkins. A truly thoughtful gift for the garden lover in your life.

materials

- ✗ **4 cotton or linen napkins**
- ✗ **1 skein each of the embroidery floss colors in the design chart**
- ✗ **Embroidery needle**
- ✗ **Embroidery hoop**
- ✗ **Scissors**

Use 3 strands of embroidery floss to stitch this project.

TIP: Don't tighten your embroidery hoop too much, as that can damage the weave of the fabric. Remove the napkin from the hoop whenever you're done stitching for the day.

1 ⟩ Transfer the designs (page 181) onto the napkins, using your favorite transfer method (page 9).

2 ⟩ Stem stitch the designs according to the charts on page 149.

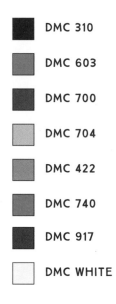

DMC 310

DMC 603

DMC 700

DMC 704

DMC 422

DMC 740

DMC 917

DMC WHITE

BUZZY BEE PENCIL CASE

Did you know that honeybees are aces at organization? Stitch up this adorable pencil case and say good-bye to scattered pens and pencils! The sweet embroidered honeybee is fun and simple to stitch and the snap closure will keep everything secure. Makes a wonderful eyeglass case, too.

materials

- ✕ **Pencil Case Front: 8″ x 4″ medium gray felt**

- ✕ **1 skein each of the embroidery floss colors in the design chart**

- ✕ **Pencil Case Lining: 9½″ x 4″ hot pink felt**

- ✕ **Pencil Case Back: 9½″ x 4″ bright yellow felt**

- ✕ **Small snap closure (in 2 parts)**

- ✕ **Scissors**

- ✕ **Straight pins**

- ✕ **Embroidery needle**

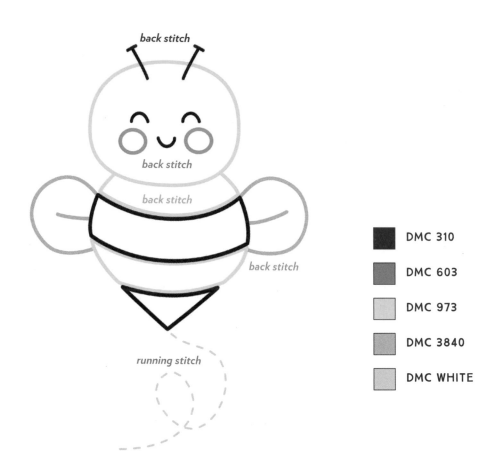

back stitch

back stitch

back stitch

back stitch

running stitch

■	DMC 310
■	DMC 603
☐	DMC 973
■	DMC 3840
■	DMC WHITE

Cut out the templates (page 182). Pin the templates to the felt pieces, and cut carefully along the lines. Once you've cut out all the felt pieces, you're ready to begin!

Use 3 strands of embroidery floss to stitch this project.

1 > Transfer the design onto the Pencil Case Front felt, using your favorite transfer method (page 9).

2 > Backstitch the design following the chart above.

3

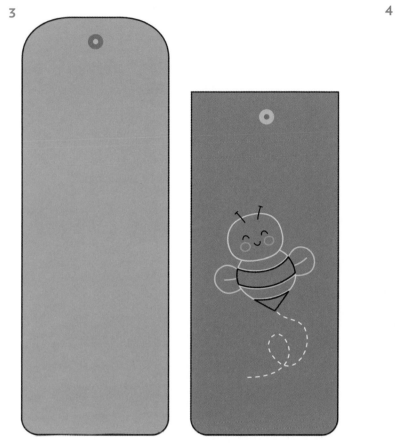

4

3 〉 Mark the positions of the snap closures on the Pencil Case Front and the Lining felt, centered and about ½″ from the top edge, as shown. Sew snap closures in place.

4 〉 Align the Pencil Case Front, the Lining, and the Pencil Case Back, and pin them together. With brightly colored thread, blanket stitch all three layers together around the outer edge.

MAGIC UNICORN WALL ART

Needle and thread are your keys to a magical world where unicorns prance in the sunshine, the grass is lush, and a bright blue castle sits on the hills beyond. If you need a break from your cares, this is just the project for you. Display this precious embroidery in a hoop to bring a sense of fairy-tale magic to any room.

materials

- One 12″ x 12″ piece of white woven cotton or linen fabric

- 1 skein each of the embroidery floss colors in the design chart

- 12″ length ribbon

- Embroidery needle

- Scissors

- 8″ embroidery hoop (for stitching)

- 7″ embroidery hoop (for framing)

Use 3 strands of embroidery floss to stitch this project.

TIP: Even though this project will use a 7″ embroidery hoop for framing, use an 8″ hoop while you stitch. When it's time to frame your design, the hoop creases will get folded over to the back.

1 > Transfer the Magic Unicorn design (page 183) onto the center of the fabric, using your favorite transfer method (page 9).

2 > Using an 8″ embroidery hoop, stitch the design following the chart on page 157.

3 > Gently iron the finished stitchwork on the opposite side of the design, being careful not to flatten the stitches. Center it in the 7″ embroidery hoop and tighten, making sure the fabric is straight and taut like a drum. Trim the excess fabric around the hoop, leaving enough to fold over to the back (about 2″). Fold the fabric to the back of the hoop and sew a simple running stitch near the outer edge, pulling firmly to gather the fabric to the back. Tie off.

4 > Tie a ribbon to the metal clamp of the hoop if you'd like and you're ready to display!

running stitch

back stitch

stem stitch

back stitch

back stitch

back stitch

back stitch

stem stitch

back stitch

stem stitch

stem stitch

stem stitch

back stitch

stem stitch

stem stitch

back stitch

back stitch

back stitch

	DMC 310		DMC 3609		DMC 741		DMC 3837
	DMC 603		DMC 601		DMC 905		DMC 415
	DMC 973		DMC 996		DMC 907		

templates

TOASTER PASTRY GIFT CARD HOLDER

Copy at 100%

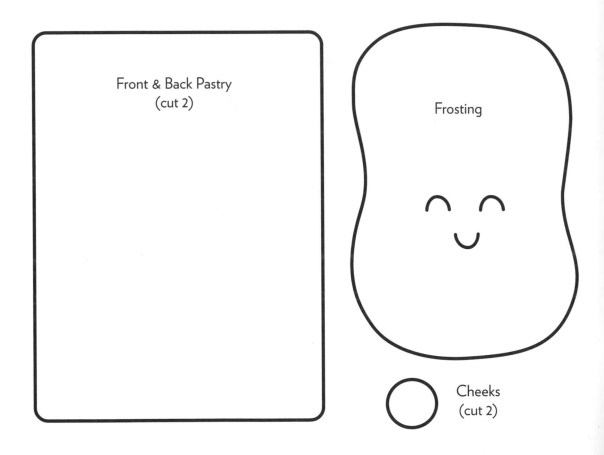

Front & Back Pastry
(cut 2)

Frosting

Cheeks
(cut 2)

RAINBOW CLOUD PLUSHIE

Copy at 200%

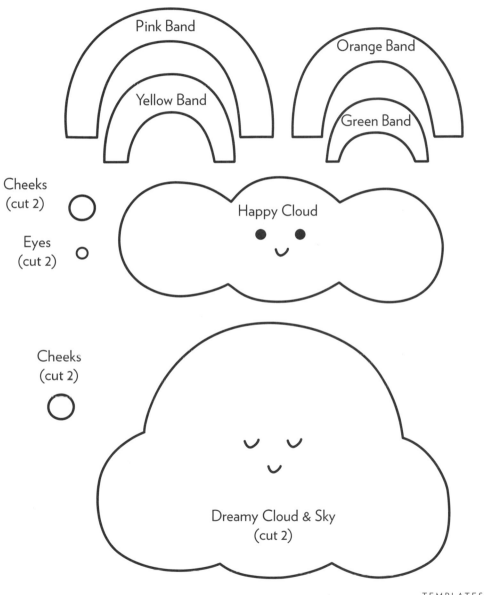

Pink Band

Orange Band

Yellow Band

Green Band

Cheeks
(cut 2)

Eyes
(cut 2)

Happy Cloud

Cheeks
(cut 2)

Dreamy Cloud & Sky
(cut 2)

FAST FOOD KEYCHAINS

Copy at 100%

HAMBURGER

Cheeks
(cut 2)

Top Bun

Lettuce

Tomato

Cheese

Patty

Bottom Bun

SHAKE

Cheeks
(cut 2)

Straw

Lid

Label

Cup

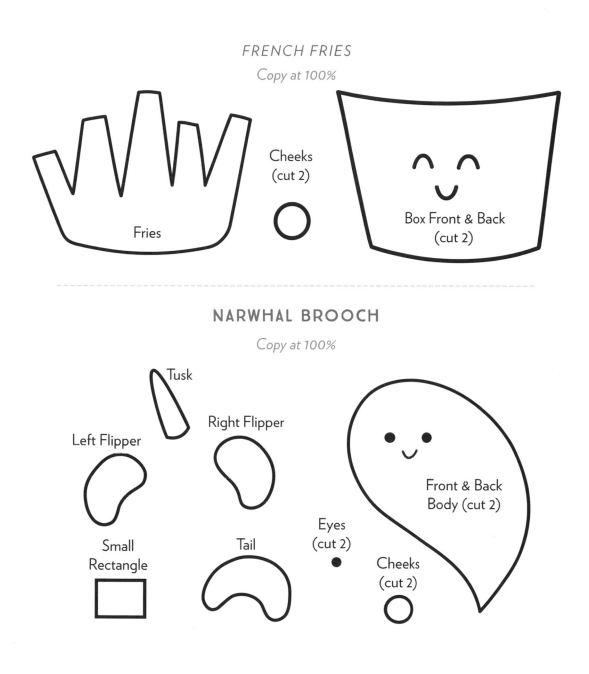

FRENCH FRIES
Copy at 100%

Fries

Cheeks
(cut 2)

Box Front & Back
(cut 2)

NARWHAL BROOCH
Copy at 100%

Tusk

Left Flipper

Right Flipper

Small
Rectangle

Tail

Eyes
(cut 2)

Front & Back
Body (cut 2)

Cheeks
(cut 2)

GLAM PINEAPPLE PLUSHIE

Copy at 100%

Pineapple Front & Back
(cut 2)

Leaves

Cheeks
(cut 2)

CUPCAKE BAG CHARM

Copy at 100%

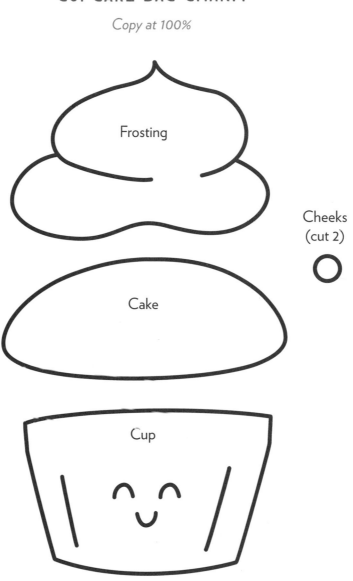

Frosting

Cheeks
(cut 2)

Cake

Cup

PAPER CLIP TOPPERS

TACO
Copy at 100%

Tomato

Taco Front & Back (cut 2)

Cheeks (cut 2)

Lettuce

Clip Cover

PIZZA
Copy at 100%

Crust

Cheeks (cut 2)

Pizza

Pepperoni Pieces

Clip Cover

LITTLE CRAB CORD KEEPER

Copy at 100%

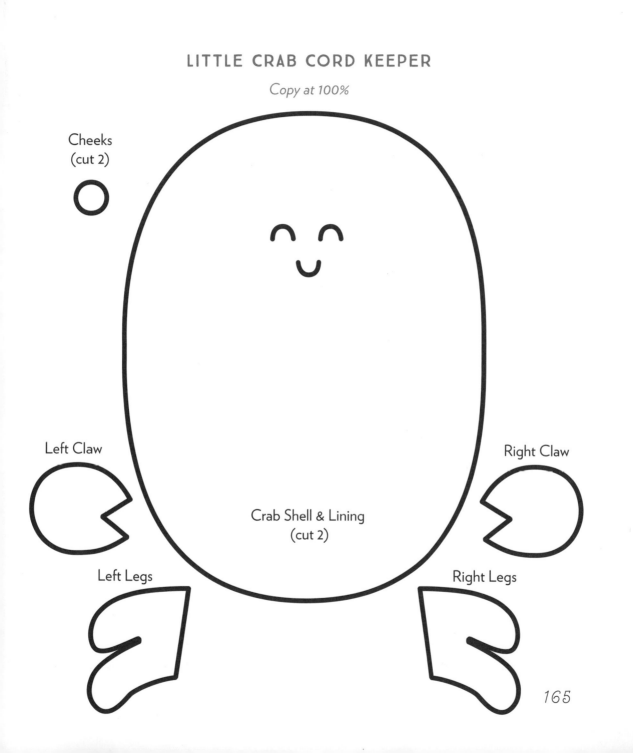

Cheeks
(cut 2)

Left Claw

Right Claw

Crab Shell & Lining
(cut 2)

Left Legs

Right Legs

FUDGE POP PLUSHIE

Copy at 133%

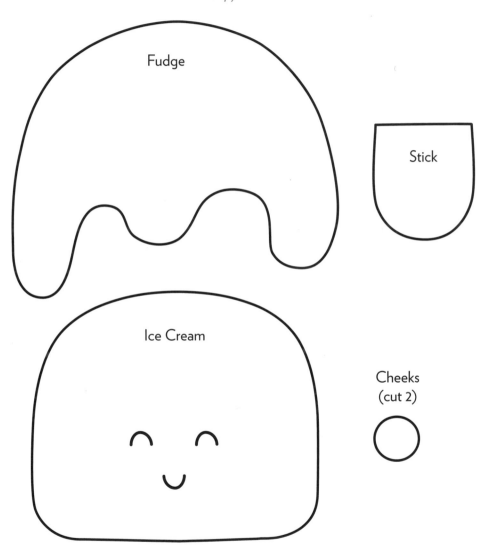

Fudge

Stick

Ice Cream

Cheeks
(cut 2)

GIRAFFE WINE BOTTLE TOPPER

Copy at 100%

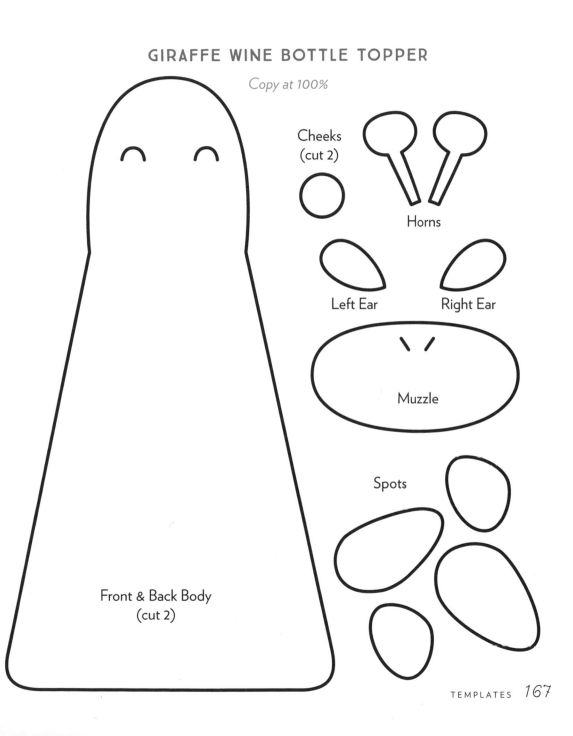

Cheeks
(cut 2)

Horns

Left Ear

Right Ear

Muzzle

Spots

Front & Back Body
(cut 2)

LITTLE LLAMA ORNAMENT

Copy at 100%

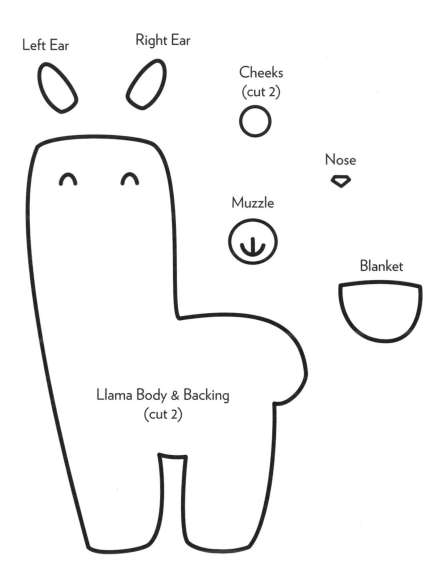

Left Ear

Right Ear

Cheeks
(cut 2)

Nose

Muzzle

Blanket

Llama Body & Backing
(cut 2)

FROSTY TREAT CHARMS

Copy at 100%

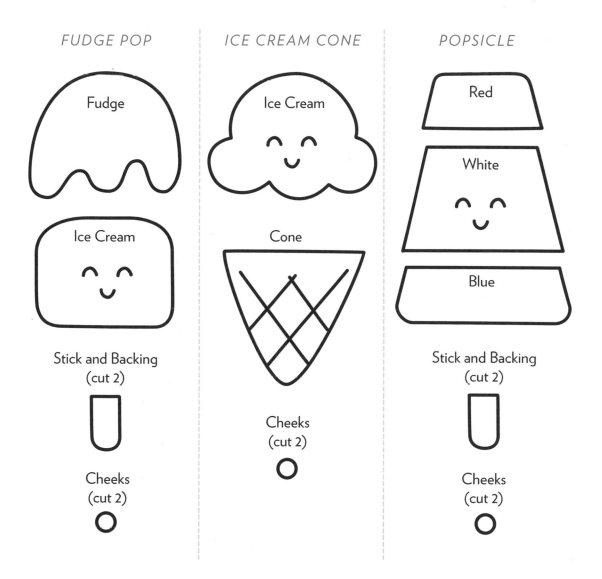

FUDGE POP

Fudge

Ice Cream

Stick and Backing
(cut 2)

Cheeks
(cut 2)

ICE CREAM CONE

Ice Cream

Cone

Cheeks
(cut 2)

POPSICLE

Red

White

Blue

Stick and Backing
(cut 2)

Cheeks
(cut 2)

SWEET SLOTH PENCIL TOPPER

Copy at 100%

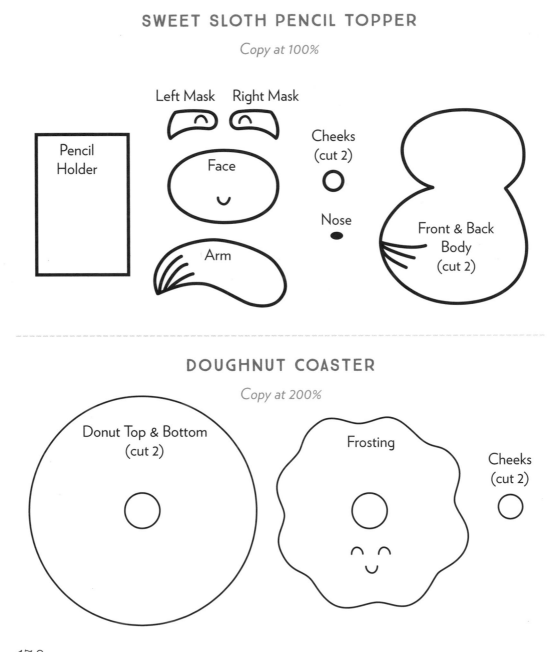

Left Mask Right Mask

Pencil Holder

Face

Cheeks (cut 2)

Nose

Arm

Front & Back Body (cut 2)

DOUGHNUT COASTER

Copy at 200%

Donut Top & Bottom (cut 2)

Frosting

Cheeks (cut 2)

WOODLAND CRITTERS GARLAND

Copy at 100%

HEDGEHOG

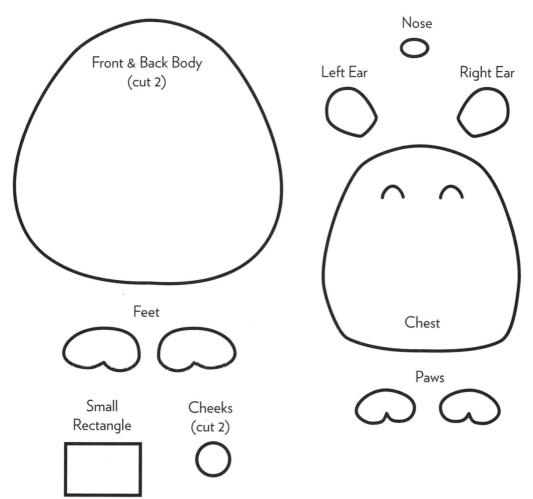

Front & Back Body
(cut 2)

Nose

Left Ear

Right Ear

Feet

Chest

Paws

Small
Rectangle

Cheeks
(cut 2)

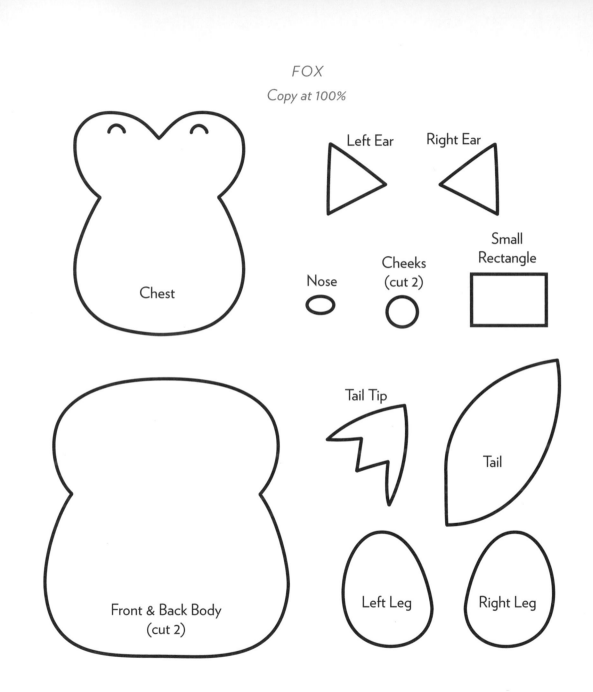

FOX

Copy at 100%

Left Ear

Right Ear

Chest

Nose

Cheeks
(cut 2)

Small
Rectangle

Tail Tip

Tail

Front & Back Body
(cut 2)

Left Leg

Right Leg

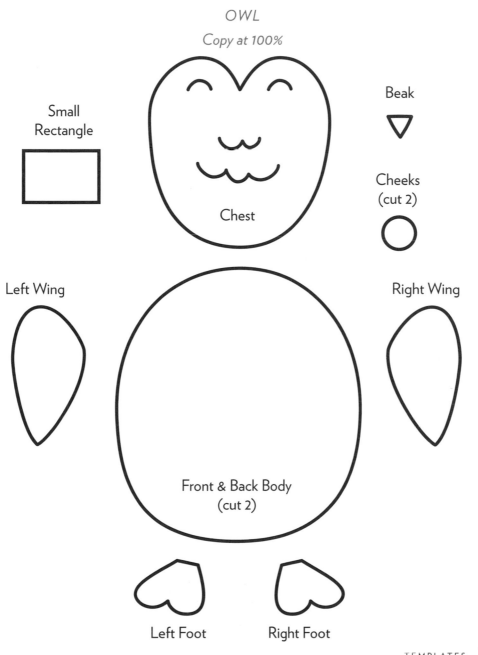

OWL

Copy at 100%

Beak

Small
Rectangle

Cheeks
(cut 2)

Chest

Left Wing

Right Wing

Front & Back Body
(cut 2)

Left Foot

Right Foot

HAPPY AVOCADO GIFT TAG

Copy at 100%

SEAL AND PENGUIN CUPCAKE TOPPERS

Copy at 100%

Gift Tag

Toothpick Holder

LUCKY ELEPHANT MINI GIFT BAG

Copy at 200%

Handles (cut 2)

Gift Bag

TOADSTOOL AND ACORN
NAPKIN RINGS

Copy at 133%

CHEERFUL BLOOMS
COIN PURSE

Copy at 200%

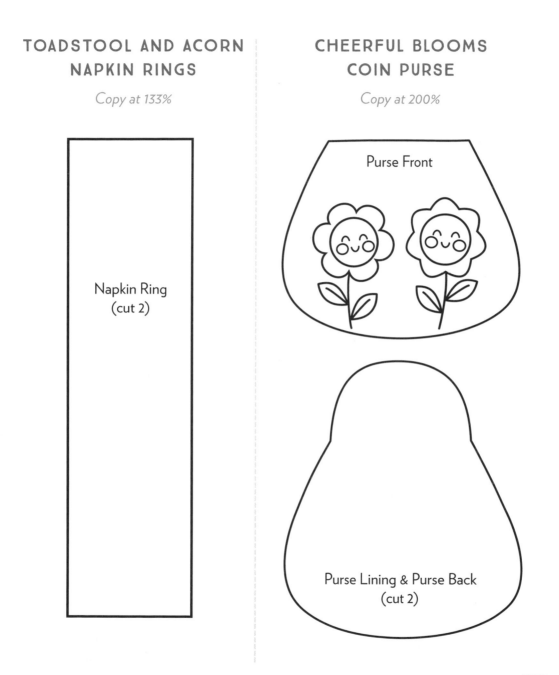

Napkin Ring
(cut 2)

Purse Front

Purse Lining & Purse Back
(cut 2)

APPLE PIE APRON

Copy at 100%

Copy at 100%

TRIP TO THE MARKET TOTE

Copy at 100%

COFFEE SHOP TREATS CUP COZY

Copy Cup Cozy at 200%

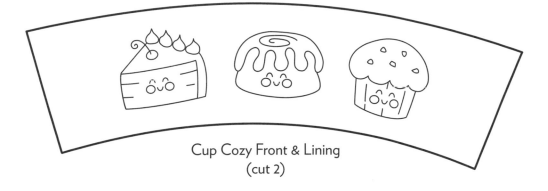

Cup Cozy Front & Lining
(cut 2)

Copy Coffee Shop Treats Patterns at 100%

DRAGON BOOKMARK

Copy at 100%

Front & Back
(cut 2)

LITTLE MONSTER ONESIE

Copy at 100%

SWEET DREAMS SLUMBER MASK

Copy at 200%

EAT YOUR VEGGIES NAPKINS

Copy at 100%

Pencil Case
Lining & Back
(cut 2)

BUZZY BEE
PENCIL CASE

Copy at 133%

Pencil Case
Front

MAGIC UNICORN WALL ART

Copy at 100%

index